"Like the classic diary, this photobiography captures the ordinariness of Anne Frank's life. The particulars personalize the sorrow of the six million gone. . . . Excerpts from Anne's diaries are combined with an account of the two years in the Secret Annex (from the time of going into hiding until the betrayal, arrest, and deportation) and also with a general history and photographs of the rise of Nazism and the fate of the Jews. . . . It's hard to know which pages are more heartbreaking: the facsimile of the last diary entry; the picture of the marks on the wall recording the growth of Anne and her sister in their hiding place; the mass scenes of the transports and concentration camps. All libraries will want this: for classroom units studying the Holocaust, for kids reading the diary, for everyone who remembers it."

—*Booklist,* starred review

"One feels the personal loss of a bright, fun-loving and talented individual . . . and also remembers that many Anne Franks died during this nightmarish period."

—*School Library Journal,* starred review

"Reminds us that Anne was real—and it's made clear that some people need reminding—but also lets us see Anne as she never could have seen herself."

—*Bulletin of the Center for Children's Books*

ALA Notable Book of the Year
An ALA Best Book for Young Adults
ALA Recommended Book for Reluctant Readers
Winner of the Christopher Award
Booklist Editor's Choice
Bulletin Blue Ribbon Book
Mildred L. Batchelder Honor Book

Anne Frank

Beyond the Diary

A Photographic Remembrance

Anne Frank.

With an Introduction by Anna Quindlen

by Ruud van der Rol and Rian Verhoeven
in association with the Anne Frank House
translated by Tony Langham and Plym Peters

PUFFIN BOOKS

PUFFIN BOOKS
Published by the Penguin Group
Penguin Books USA Inc., 375 Hudson Street, New York, New York 10014, U.S.A.
Penguin Books Ltd, 27 Wrights Lane, London W8 5TZ, England
Penguin Books Australia Ltd, Ringwood, Victoria, Australia
Penguin Books Canada Ltd, 10 Alcorn Avenue, Toronto, Ontario, Canada M4V 3B2
Penguin Books (N.Z.) Ltd, 182-190 Wairau Road, Auckland 10, New Zealand

Penguin Books Ltd, Registered Offices: Harmondsworth, Middlesex, England

First published in the United States of America by Viking,
a division of Penguin Books USA Inc., 1993

Published in Puffin Books, 1995

9 10 8

Translation copyright © Anne Frank Stichting, Amsterdam, 1993
Introduction copyright © Anna Quindlen, 1993

Originally published in the Netherlands by La Riviere & Voorhoeven,
© Anne Frank Stichting, Amsterdam, 1992
All rights reserved

THE LIBRARY OF CONGRESS HAS CATALOGED THE VIKING EDITION AS FOLLOWS:

Verhoeven, Rian. Anne Frank, beyond the diary:
a photographic remembrance / by Ruud van der Rol and Rian Verhoeven.   p.   cm.
Summary: Photographs, illustrations, and maps accompany historical essays, diary excerpts,
and interviews, providing an insight to Anne Frank and the massive upheaval which tore apart her world.
ISBN 0-670-84932-4
1. Frank, Anne, 1929–1945—Pictorial works—Juvenile literature.
2. Jews—Netherlands—Amsterdam—Biography—Pictorial works—Juvenile literature.
3. Holocaust, Jewish (1939–1945)—Netherlands—Amsterdam—Pictorial works—Juvenile literature.
4. Amsterdam (Netherlands)—Biography—Pictorial works—Juvenile literature.
[1. Frank, Anne, 1929–1945. 2. Jews—Biography.
3. Holocaust, Jewish (1939–1945)—Netherlands—Amsterdam.]   I. Title.
DS135.N6F7385   1993   940.53'18'092—dc20   [B]   92-41528   CIP   AC

Puffin Books ISBN 0-14-036926-0

Printed in Hong Kong
Set in New Baskerville

Acknowledgments

Photographic research
Yt Stoker

Photography
Allard Bovenberg
Kees Rutten
Maarten van de Velde

Maps and drawing of the Secret Annex
Gerard de Groot

Map on page 30
Andrew Mudryk

Editing
Stephanie Hutter

Design
Jo Metsch

With thanks to: David Barnouw of the Netherlands State Institute for War Documentation, Karen Beijer, Janrense Boonstra, Anki Duin, Miep Gies, Yoeri de Graaf, Sonja Lukkenaer, Inge Luttikhuizen, Trudie van Nimwegen, Karen Peters, Marie-José Rijnders, Wouter van der Sluis, Juliëtte Smink, Dineke Stam, Tim Steinweg, Anna Westra, and Hans Westra.

With special thanks to: Joke Kniesmeyer.
Her expertise and her excellent teamwork were invaluable in the creation of this book.

Contents

Maps appear on pages 12–13, 30, 46, 83, 94–95

Introduction

In the forty-six years since it was first published and the fifty since it was written, the diary of Anne Frank has taken on a kind of mystical quality for the adolescents who first encounter it and the adults left with its spiritual aftertaste. I read the diary first when I was twelve, reread it just last week, as a companion work to the photographs in this book. Its power is so enormous that, looking at the pictures of the actual diary, with its plaid cover and impotent little lock, a shiver took hold of me as though the thing was a relic, as indeed it is.

Now wife and mother, even-keeled and middle-aged, all those things that Anne never had a chance to be, I cannot read it without feeling the pall, the enormous tragedy that hangs over the entire enterprise, whose essence is contained unadorned in the final sentence of the epilogue: "In March 1945, two months before the liberation of Holland, Anne died in the concentration camp at Bergen-Belsen."

The struggle for identity, the fears, the doubts, above all the everydayness in the diary entries, the worries about outgrown shoes, the romantic yearnings, and the ever-present conflicts with Mama and Margot reflect, mirror, and elevate the lives of millions who went about the business of studying, romancing, cooking, sewing, and struggling to live in the world until the Nazis ended their millions of ordinary, individual lives.

The photograph of Anne Frank that most of us know best, the one on the cover of the paperback edition of the book in which she gazes slightly upward, her mouth somewhat tremulous, her eyes black holes, is as powerful an evocation of teetering on the edge of mortality as any I ever encountered as a girl.

And yet mortality is not what younger readers recognize when they read the diary. Quite the contrary: Anne's odyssey of self-interrogation within the claustrophobic confines of the Secret Annex becomes an extraordinary metaphor for life, in particular for the life of the adolescent, bursting to be free while trapped in a close net of family, friends, and constant scrutiny, real and imagined. Any thirteen-year-old can instantly understand Anne's feelings in the first few pages, when she says she will call her diary Kitty because she really has no bosom friend—"just fun and joking, nothing more."

From time to time she talks about the horrors beyond her window, but most of the diary is about the turmoil within her growing heart. Cooped up, misunderstood, she is every teenager when she bursts out, halfway through her time in hiding, "Would anyone, either Jew or non-Jew, understand this about me, that I am simply a young girl badly in need of some rollicking fun?" In the foreword Eleanor Roosevelt wrote at the time of the U.S. publication of the diary, she referred to the "horror and humiliation" of the Franks' existence. But horror and humiliation are the grown-up vision of what comes after for Anne, not the reality of her life in the Annex, where she spends her time trying to figure out who will love her as she is and how she will make do with last year's undervests.

Reading this book as an adult, I am inevitably shadowed by the specter of Anne's future, of how all these concerns will evaporate before what is still to come. Reading it at twelve, I thought only of the present—my present, Anne's present, and the similarities between them.

But the past, Anne's past, has been shadowy for many of us until now, and oh, what a great relief it is to see the pictures here. And how far they go toward providing her, these many years later, the courtesy of fusing the icon and the ordinary girl. The classic foreshadowing photograph gives way to many other Annes, laughing, shy, open-faced, baby, toddler, almost adolescent; above all, one of her walking down the street in the sunlight, grinning, before the diary, before the attic.

We know Anne Frank the victim and Anne Frank the fugitive. This is Anne Frank the free, the living, the person who was able to write what has become a life lesson for millions of us in the years since: "In spite of everything I still believe that people are really good at heart."

There is something so humanizing about these photographs. In them Anne has not yet passed into historical legend. In them the Annex becomes a building again, narrow and unprepossessing. We see the diary with all its teenage blemishes, not transcribed neatly on the page but pocked with pasted pictures, scribbled and hap-hazard, the work of a girl, not a symbol, not a metaphor.

Here we see the real epilogue, too, in its terrible simplicity: a long list of "Judentransport," and halfway down, entry number 309, "Frank . . . . Anneliese."

As we grew, and as the legend grew as well, Anne Frank had in some essential way ceased to be an ordinary person. These pictures make her whole again: one little Jewish girl, one life growing, thriving, struggling to break the surface of its soil like a seedling just at the time that the soil was poisoned. The failed flowering means more with the seeds. Seeing the baby Anne, the smiling Anne, the free Anne, makes her life all that much more ordinary. And that much more heroic and heartbreaking.

—Anna Quindlen

Anne Frank

Beyond the Diary

The Best Birthday Present

Anne Frank woke at six o'clock in the morning on Friday, June 12. She could hardly wait to get out of bed. That she was up so early was not surprising, since today was her thirteenth birthday.

It was wartime, 1942. Anne was living with her father and mother and her sister, Margot, who was three years older than Anne, in a housing development in Amsterdam, the capital city of the Netherlands. The Netherlands had been occupied for two years by the Germans, who had launched a campaign of discrimination and persecution against the Jews. It was becoming increasingly difficult for Jews such as the Frank family to lead ordinary lives, but Anne was not thinking about that on her birthday.

At seven o'clock Anne went to her parents' bedroom. Then the whole family gathered in the living room to unwrap Anne's presents.

Anne received many gifts that day, including books, a jigsaw puzzle, a brooch, and candy. But her best present was one given by her parents that morning: a hardcover diary, bound in red and white checkered cloth. She had never had a diary before and was delighted with the gift. Anne had many friends, both boys and girls, but with them she talked only about everyday things. But now Anne's diary would be her very best friend, a friend she could trust with everything. She called her new friend "Kitty."

On the first page of her diary Anne wrote: *I hope I shall be able to confide in you completely, as I have never been able to do in anyone before, and I hope that you will be a great support and comfort to me. Anne Frank* (June 12, 1942)

Ik zal hoop ik aan jou alles kunnen toevertrouwen, zoals ik het nog aan niemand gekend heb, en ik hoop dat je een grote steun van me zult zijn. Anne Frank. 12 Juni 1942.

On the inside of the cover she stuck a photograph of herself and wrote next to it: *Gorgeous photograph isn't it!!!!*

Anne started writing to Kitty in her diary two days later, on Sunday, June 14. She would continue filling it for just over two years with her thoughts and feelings, and stories about all the things that happened to her. But on that first day, she could not suspect how her life was suddenly to change completely. Nor could she imagine that later millions of people throughout the world would read her diary.

From Frankfurt to Amsterdam

Anne Frank was born in the German city of Frankfurt am Main on June 12, 1929. Her father took this photograph of Anne and her mother, Edith Frank-Holländer, the following day. A keen photographer, Otto Frank took many photographs, especially of his children, and started a photo album for Anne.

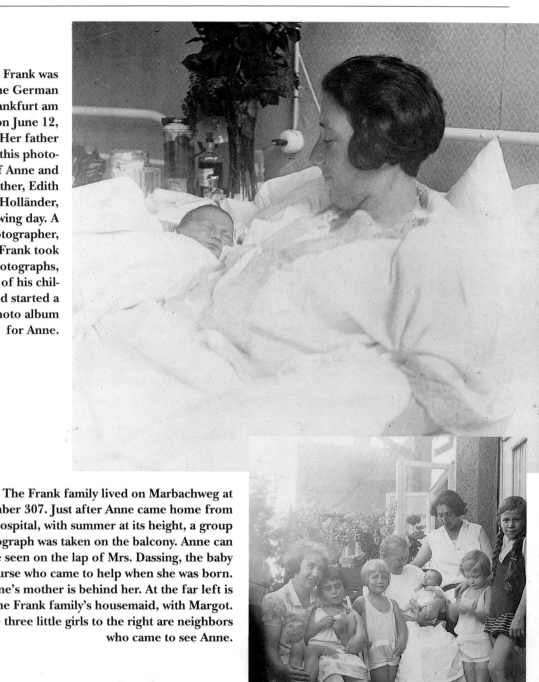

The Frank family lived on Marbachweg at number 307. Just after Anne came home from the hospital, with summer at its height, a group photograph was taken on the balcony. Anne can be seen on the lap of Mrs. Dassing, the baby nurse who came to help when she was born. Anne's mother is behind her. At the far left is Kathi, the Frank family's housemaid, with Margot. The three little girls to the right are neighbors who came to see Anne.

When Anne was born, her parents had been married for four years. The Frank family was Jewish, and Otto and Edith were married in a synagogue on May 12, 1925. The wedding took place in Aachen, very near the Dutch border, where Edith Holländer had been born. Otto was thirty-six years old, Edith twenty-five. The newlyweds went to Italy for their honeymoon. Here they are in San Remo on the Mediterranean coast, one of several places where they stayed.

Members of the Frank family soon came to visit and admire the new baby, and Otto Frank was there with his camera. Here Anne's grandmother poses with her two grandchildren: newborn Anne and her older sister, Margot, born on February 16, 1926.

Otto, Edith, and Margot lived on the first two floors in the right half of this house. Otto and Edith had chosen this new home because they wanted a house with a garden.

Otto's mother was Alice Frank-Stern. His father had died in 1909, when Otto was only twenty years old. Otto Frank was born and grew up in Frankfurt am Main, where his family had lived for generations. Otto and Edith lived in Otto's mother's house for over two years. Then, in the autumn of 1927, when Margot was eighteen months old, they moved to the house on Marbachweg.

There were many children living in the Franks' new neighborhood, and they came to play with Margot in the garden almost every afternoon. Margot can be seen here on the far left. Anne was still in her cradle at the time, but she later wrote the date above this picture in her photograph album: "July 1929."

As soon as Anne could walk she played with the other children. Just over a year later, in September 1930, Anne can also be seen in a photograph. She is the third child from the left (wearing a hat), and Margot is third from the right. The children in the neighborhood all had different religious backgrounds. Whether Catholic, Protestant, or Jewish, they shared a curiosity about each other's religious holidays. Margot was invited to the communion celebration of one of her girlfriends, and the neighbors' children were sometimes invited to join the Frank family's celebration of Hanukkah.

The Frank family were Reform Jews, which means that they observed the traditions of the Jewish religion without strictly adhering to all Jewish beliefs and customs. The Frank family was German, spoke German, and read German. Reading and studying were very important to Otto Frank, not only for himself, but also for his daughters. This photograph shows Margot in front of his bookcase in 1929.

"Papa with his kids" was the caption Anne later wrote in her photograph album for this picture (1930). Anne and Margot were crazy about their father, and even had a pet name for him. Along with their mother, they usually called him "Pim." Later Anne often used this name to refer to her father in her diary.

Before going to bed at night, Otto frequently invented stories for Anne and Margot, usually featuring two girls named Paula. One Paula was good and obeyed her parents, while the other Paula was disobedient and always got into mischief.

At the end of March 1931, the Frank family moved again, this time to a street called Ganghoferstrasse, at number 24. Their new home had more to offer the children, from lovely walking paths through the neighborhood to hills where they could go tobogganing in the winter. Here Anne is in one of her favorite places, the sandbox in her garden. While Anne was not allowed to leave the garden, Margot was free to play with her friends in the street.

Anne and Margot continued to see their former neighbors, and soon made new friends as well. In the summer of 1932, Margot (center) and Anne (right) had just celebrated Anne's second birthday.

WHERE ANNE FRANK LIVED

Frankfurt am Main, Germany
Anne Frank was born here on June 12, 1929, and remained in this city through the spring of 1933.

Aachen, Germany
Anne, her mother, and her sister stayed here with Anne's grandmother from the summer of 1933 through the beginning of 1934. During this time, Anne's father, Otto, was in Amsterdam, looking for his family's new home.

Amsterdam, the Netherlands
Anne moved to Amsterdam in February 1934. The Frank family went into hiding in the Secret Annex on the Prinsengracht Canal on July 6, 1942. They were arrested by the Germans on August 4, 1944.

Westerbork, the Netherlands
In August 1944, Anne and her family were sent to this concentration camp, to which most Dutch Jews were deported. Anne stayed here until September 1944.

Auschwitz-Birkenau, Poland
At the beginning of September 1944, Anne and her family were taken by closed train to the concentration camp here.

Bergen-Belsen, Germany
Anne and her sister, Margot, were transferred here from Auschwitz-Birkenau at the end of 1944. They both died in this concentration camp in March 1945.

Riga

LATVIA

LITHUANIA

THE SOVIET UNION

POLAND

Warsaw

AUSCHWITZ-BIRKENAU

CZECHOSLOVAKIA

Vienna

HUNGARY

Budapest

ROMANIA

YUGOSLAVIA

Belgrade

Also Mentioned in This Book

Basel, Switzerland
In 1933, Alice Frank-Stern, Anne's grandmother, moved here from Frankfurt am Main. After the war, Otto Frank also came to live in this city.

Osnabrück, Germany
The Van Pels family, who hid in the Secret Annex with the Frank family, lived here before fleeing to Amsterdam in 1937.

KEY

▲ concentration camp

╫╫╫╫ railway line

▇ capital city

places where Anne Frank lived

● other cities

The countries on this map were drawn with their 1939 borders.

It was March 10, 1933. The worst of the winter cold had passed and the Frank family was going shopping in town. Anne and Margot are seen wearing knee socks instead of stockings, though they still have on their thick winter coats. Otto Frank took this photograph on the Hauptwache, a famous square in the center of Frankfurt am Main.

That winter the Frank family had seen many changes, as had all Jews in Germany. In January, six weeks before this picture was taken, Adolf Hitler had come to power. The news deeply troubled Otto and Edith, though they did not share their concern with their children.

In the Tietz department store near the Hauptwache was a photograph booth where Anne and Margot posed with their mother. The photograph also shows the date and the combined weight of Edith Frank and her children, almost 110 kilos, or just over 240 pounds. This is one of the last photographs taken of the Frank family in Frankfurt am Main.

Three days later, on March 13, 1933, elections were held in Frankfurt for the municipal council. Hitler's party, the Nazis, received a large share of the votes and celebrated their victory in front of the town hall, not far from the Hauptwache. Raising their arms in the Nazi salute, they screamed, "Heil Hitler! Heil Hitler! Down with the Jews!" The Nazis swarmed into the town hall and raised their flag, a black swastika on a blood-red field. The mayor was forced to resign and a Nazi took his place. The police did nothing. Similar scenes were occurring all across Germany.

Adolf Hitler Comes to Power

Adolf Hitler, leader of the Nazi Party, making a speech.

By the year Anne Frank was born, 1929, life in Germany had become very hard. Poverty and unemployment were at an all-time high, and most Germans were very dissatisfied with their government. A new party founded in 1920 called the German National Socialist Labor Party (NSDAP) was attracting increasing numbers of followers.

The leader of this organization, which was commonly known as the Nazi Party (derived from the German word *NAtionalsoZIalistische*), was Adolf Hitler. Hitler believed that the German people were a superior race, stronger, more intelligent, and better than any other people in the world. Hitler promised that once this race regained control of the government and of the lands in other countries that Germany needed to survive and prosper, the German people would enjoy a beautiful future.

And who was responsible for the problems that now gripped Germany? In ranting speeches Hitler blamed the Jews, a degenerate race that was evil, dishonest, and dangerous to all Germans. This use of anti-Semitism was not new. Throughout history, Jews had been persecuted and discriminated against, and anti-Semitism still exists in countries around the world. But in 1929 this prejudice won strong support from people desperate to find a scapegoat for their troubles and to believe in their own power again.

By 1933 the Nazi Party was the largest party in Germany and Hitler was appointed to head the government. Now the real aims of the Nazis became clear. All parties except the Nazis were banned, democracy in Germany ceased to exist, and Hitler took control of every aspect of daily life in Germany. Anyone who opposed him was beaten or imprisoned. Soon the prisons were so overcrowded that new ones, called concentration camps, had to be built. These camps, heavily guarded and surrounded by high barbed-wire fences (usually electrified), were almost impossible to escape from. They held large numbers of prisoners "concentrated" in small areas and living under inhuman conditions. Many Germans who opposed Hitler's policies kept quiet out of fear. But many more admired and blindly followed Hitler.

Hitler continued to inflame hatred of the Jews, launching a campaign of anti-Semitism on the radio, in newspapers, in films and more. He enacted laws against Jews, segregating Jewish schoolchildren, depriving Jews of jobs and property. And this was only the beginning.

On the night of November 9–10, 1938, Nazis throughout Germany went on a rampage, burning and smashing Jewish-owned shops and synagogues. That night was called "Kristallnacht," Crystal Night or the Night of Broken Glass. In the days that followed, about 30,000 Jewish men and boys were rounded up and taken to concentration camps.

In 1933, Anne, Margot, and Edith went to live with Edith's mother in Aachen. With Hitler taking more and more measures against the Jews, the Frank family feared what the future might hold if they stayed in Germany. When Otto Frank received an offer to start a new company in Amsterdam, the family decided to move to the Netherlands. These photographs were taken by a photographer in Aachen, and were probably sent to Otto Frank. By this time, he had already been in Amsterdam for a few months, starting up the business and looking for a new house.

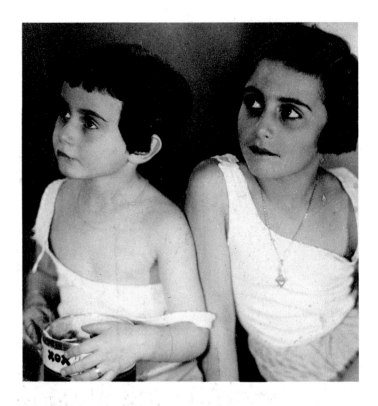

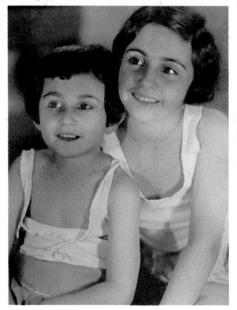

Anne's other grandmother also left Germany in 1933, moving to Switzerland, where some of her family lived. This photo was taken at the train station in Basel, Switzerland, in 1936. Anne's grandmother Alice Frank-Stern is standing on the far left; her aunt and uncle, Leni Elias-Frank and Erich Elias, are on the right; standing in between are two of Anne's cousins, Bernd and Stephan.

Fleeing to Another Country

Jewish children on their way to England. Many parents sent their children on ahead to safer countries, though the parents themselves would often be turned away, forced to remain in Germany.

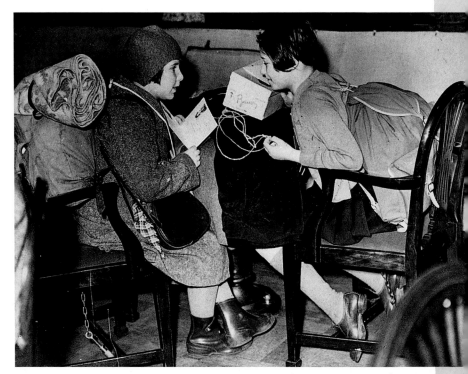

The Frank family left Germany when Hitler came to power in 1933. Otto Frank, like thousands of others now fleeing Germany, was worried about the events taking place in his country. With the rising anti-Semitism, these new refugees suspected that for them life in Germany would become intolerable. However, many more decided to wait and see what Hitler would do next, hoping things would turn out all right. But the Nazis kept introducing more measures against their opponents and Jews. New laws were passed depriving them of their work, their money, and their freedom.

Over the next few years, thousands of German Jews tried to escape to other countries. But this became more difficult every day. Refugees needed money, both for their journey and to gain entry into their new countries, many of which demanded that they already have jobs or their own income. But with Hitler taking control of Jewish businesses, this was often impossible. The governments of many countries, believing that the stories of persecution and the horrible conditions in concentration camps were exaggerated, began putting increasing restrictions on refugees. Some stopped accepting them altogether. Nevertheless, roughly 300,000 people, about half of the Jewish population, managed to escape Germany between 1933 and 1939.

Those who had no money, were too old or sick to travel, or could not pass the regulations for admittance, had to remain in Germany. For them, life became a nightmare. Humiliated on the streets and in school, deprived of their livelihoods, they saw every freedom taken away step by step, until they had no rights at all.

The station in Naarden. These Jewish refugees have just arrived in the Netherlands.

Otto Frank found his family's new home in the autumn of 1933: the third floor of a house on the Merwedeplein in Amsterdam. Their home (highlighted in red) was part of a new housing complex; you can see the small trees and shrubs recently planted in the neighborhood green. Edith and Margot joined Otto in Amsterdam in December, though Anne stayed on with her grandmother until the house had been completely furnished. Nine years later, Anne wrote about her arrival in her diary: *Margot went on to Holland in December, and I followed in February, and was put on Margot's table as a birthday present.*

This would be the Frank family's home until they went into hiding.

Over the next year, many new houses were built in the complex, much to the delight of the children. With the continuous construction, there were always large piles of sand to play in, which for Anne (five years old in this picture) was a great improvement over her old sandbox in Frankfurt. The Frank family liked living in their new neighborhood, where several other Jewish families had also fled from Germany.

One of the advantages of Amsterdam was that it was not far from the shore. The Frank family regularly spent the holidays at the beach in Zandvoort aan Zee, where they are pictured in the summer of 1934. Mrs. Schneider, who was Otto Frank's secretary in Frankfurt, is sitting in the beach chair, with Anne at her feet, and Margot and Edith to the left and right.

Anne often played with her friends in the street, which wasn't dangerous since few people had cars. This photograph was taken in 1936 on the sidewalk of the neighborhood square, and shows Anne (right), now seven years old, with two of her friends, Eva Goldberg (left) and Sanne Ledermann (center).

Anne began her schooling in 1934. She attended a Montessori school near Merwedeplein, where Margot also went. After two years of preschool, she moved on to regular gradeschool classes. Here Anne (in red square) is seen with her classmates and their teacher, Mr. Van Gelder. Only seven years old, Anne was already reading and writing quite well.

As soon as Anne and Margot could write, they sent letters and greeting cards to members of their family and to their old friends in Frankfurt am Main, and to their former housekeeper, Kathi. This card was sent by Anne to her former neighbor Gertrud in 1937, when Anne was visiting her grandmother in Aachen. Anne remembered that Gertrud did not know any Dutch, so she wrote simply "Deine Anne," German for "Your Anne."

The company Otto Frank began in Amsterdam in 1933 was called Opekta-Works. It sold pectin, a powdered fruit extract used to make jam. The front of the label reads, "Jams and Jellies in 10 Minutes." Opekta ran a telephone information service from Otto's office for customers who had questions about making jam. All calls were handled by Miep Santrouschitz, until she was joined by Bep Voskuijl after the summer of 1937.

Miep Santrouschitz and Otto Frank. Miep shared Otto's fierce opposition to Hitler and the Nazis, and frequently discussed what was happening in Germany with him. A strong friendship grew between Miep and the Frank family, whom she regularly visited with her fiancé, Jan Gies.

This photo, taken in 1936, shows the truck used to advertise Opekta, driving through the streets of Amsterdam.

Here Anne is on the sidewalk outside her father's office, which she would occasionally visit. While Otto and Miep discussed politics, Anne preferred to talk to Miep about movies and movie stars.

Otto Frank started a second company, Pectacon B.V., in 1938, selling herbs for seasoning meat. His partner was Hermann van Pels, who had fled from Osnabrück, Germany, with his family the year before. He had one son, Peter, pictured here (center) with his friends in Osnabrück in 1935 or 1936 when he was eight or nine years old.

The Frank family went to the photographer nearly every year to have a sheet of passport photos taken. With dozens of pictures on each sheet, the sessions provided a lively record of the Frank girls' growth. These are some of Margot's photographs for 1939.

Margot was quieter than Anne and much more attentive to her parents. She also took better care of her clothes, and was often held up as an example to Anne by her parents. Sometimes Anne was jealous of Margot because she was so good at school—and because some people said that Margot was smarter and prettier than her sister.

Grandmother Holländer's passport. By March 1939, the situation for Jews in Germany had become intolerable, and Grandmother Holländer left Aachen to live with the Frank family. The hatred and violence against Jews had been growing steadily, as had Hitler's power in Europe. Many Jewish refugees from Germany were sent back at the Netherlands border, and it was a miracle that Granny was allowed through. Now ill and weak, Granny had to spend most of her time in bed.

Below are some of Anne's studio photos for (from left to right) May 1935 and December 1935, 1939, and 1940. Later Anne used these pictures to decorate her diary.

Anne in 1939. Anne's interests now were laughing, history, movie stars, Greek mythology, writing, cats, dogs, and boys. She had a large circle of friends and enjoyed going to parties with them and to the ice-cream parlor called Oasis in her neighborhood. Anne rode her bike to school every day, where she often got into trouble for talking in class with her friends, a habit which earned her a lot of extra homework.

When Anne put this photograph in her diary, she wrote underneath: *This is June 1939. . . . Margot and I had just got out of the water and I still remember how terribly cold I was, that's why I put on my bathrobe, granny sitting there at the back so sweetly and peacefully. Just as she was wont to do.*

This was one of Margot and Anne's last trips to the beach. On May 10, 1940, Hitler invaded the Netherlands. The German Army had caught up with the Frank family and there was no place left for them to flee.

At first, the German occupation did not seem too bad for the Jews in the Netherlands. Anne and Margot went to school as usual and continued to play with their old friends. Newspapers became increasingly filled with articles ridiculing Jews, but Otto and Edith tried to keep this from their daughters as much as possible.

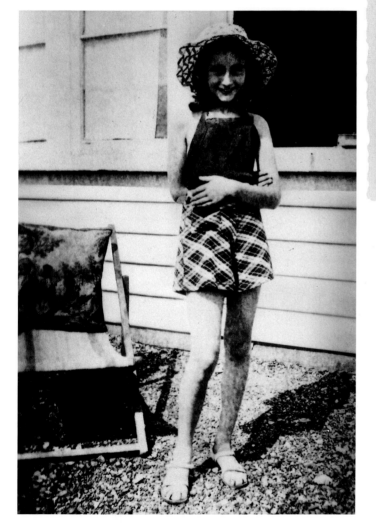

The summer of 1940. Anne is on the flat roof at the back of her house, where she often sat and read when the weather permitted. Little had changed in Holland since the occupation, except that foreign soldiers now filled the streets. But they behaved impeccably most of the time. However, secret preparations were now being made for dealing with Dutch Jews.

29

The Netherlands Is Occupied, the Persecution Begins

■ **Germany in 1942**

□ **German allies**

▦ **Axis-occupied territory**

From 1942 to 1944, Germany continued its invasion of Europe and expanded its campaigns into North Africa and the Soviet Union; Germany was supported by Italy and Japan, known collectively as the Axis powers. They were opposed by the Allies, which included the United States, England, France, and the Soviet Union.

The sign in the window says "Forbidden to Jews." Such signs appeared throughout the Netherlands under the German occupation.

While the Frank family lived a fairly trouble-free life in the Netherlands, Hitler and his supporters went ahead with their plans in Germany. In 1933 Hitler began preparing the country for war. In 1938, the German Army occupied Austria and parts of Czechoslovakia. When Germany invaded Poland in September 1939, England and France declared war. Yet the German advance continued, reaching the Netherlands on May 10, 1940. The Dutch government and the Royal Family fled to England. After the bombing of Rotterdam on May 14, which killed almost one thousand civilians, and the Germans' threat to bomb other cities, the Netherlands surrendered.

After the first few weeks of shock and panic, daily life for most people returned to normal. In the first year of the occupation, people went to work and attended school as usual, feeling that life was little changed under German rule.

It was different for Jews. At the end of 1940, all Dutch people had to register with the authorities, so the Germans knew the names and addresses of all Dutch Jews. In November 1940, all Jewish civil servants were dismissed. The following year, all Dutch citizens were given an identity card, a sort of internal passport. The cards of Jews were stamped with a "J." With every Jew now easily identifiable, the same laws which had been enacted against Jews in Germany were steadily introduced in the Netherlands.

How did the non-Jewish population in the Netherlands respond? Most people did not oppose the new restrictions. Some were afraid of the German reaction. Others didn't think the measures were serious enough to risk defying. Most just hoped the war would soon be over.

In the meantime, many people stopped associating with Jews, fearing this was too dangerous. And that was exactly what the Germans wanted. As more anti-Jewish measures were passed, the people who could have helped the Jews let them grow isolated, while the Jews became powerless to help themselves. But what was the ultimate goal of these measures? That was a carefully kept secret.

From May 1942, all Jews aged six and above had to wear a yellow Star of David with the word "Jew" written in the middle, one of the measures designed to identify and isolate Jews.

Anne on the balcony of her house on Merwedeplein in May 1941. Anne later wrote in her album under this photograph:

Granny was supposed to be on the photograph. Margot pressed down the shutter and when it was developed we saw that Granny had disappeared.

On December 1, 1940, Otto Frank's business moved to number 263 on the Prinsengracht Canal. This photograph of the office staff was taken the next year. In the foreground, from left to right, are Bep Voskuijl and Miep Santrouschitz. In the background are Esther and Pine, who only worked in the office for a short time.

By now, Holland had been occupied by the Germans for almost six months. Otto knew that in Germany, Jews had been forced to give up their businesses. Expecting the same measure to be ordered in Holland, he transferred the ownership of his business to Victor Kugler and Johannes Kleiman in 1941. The business was now renamed Trading Company Gies & Co.

Anne at the Montessori school in 1941, her last year in grade school. After the summer holidays in 1941, Jewish children learned that they would no longer be allowed to go to the school of their choice. From then on, schools were segregated between Jewish and non-Jewish children. Anne and Margot now went to a Jewish school with only Jewish teachers.

But this was only the beginning. Anne later wrote in her diary:

There have been all sorts of Jewish laws. Jews must wear a yellow star; Jews must hand in their bicycles. Jews are banned from trams and are forbidden to use any car, even a private one; Jews are only allowed to do their shopping between three and five o'clock, and then only in shops which bear the placard Jewish Shop; Jews may only use Jewish barbers; Jews must be indoors from eight o'clock in the evening until six o'clock in the morning. . . .

But life went on in spite of it all. Jacque used to say to me: "You're scared to do anything because it may be forbidden."

On July 16, 1941, Miep married Jan Gies and the Frank family was invited to the wedding. Here Otto and Anne are walking with other wedding guests. Edith Frank had stayed at home with Granny Holländer, who was very ill. Granny did not live long. Anne wrote: . . . *in the summer of 1941 Granny Holländer fell very ill, she had to have an operation and my birthday didn't mean much. . . . Granny died this winter 1941–1942. And no one will ever know how much she is in my thoughts and how much I love her still.*

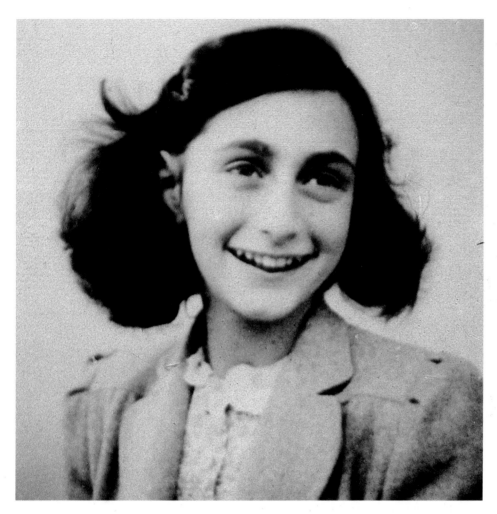

It was June 1942. *It is boiling hot, we are all positively melting and in this heat I have to go on foot everywhere. Now I can fully appreciate how nice a tram is, but that is a forbidden luxury for Jews. Shank's pony is good enough for us. . . . We are allowed to go on the ferry and that is about all, there is a little boat from the Jozef Israëlskade, where the man took us at once when we asked him.*

Anne and Margot often played Ping-Pong with their friends, usually following the game with a trip to one of the ice-cream parlors where Jews were still permitted.

VAKKEN	STAND VAN KENNIS				OPMERKINGEN omtrent vorderingen, vlijt en gedrag. (Deze kolommen worden slechts ingevuld als daartoe bepaalde aanleiding bestaat).			
	1	2	3	4	Eerste rapport	Tweede rapport	Derde rapport	Jaarrapport
Stelkunde	9	8	8	9				
Gonio- en Trigonometrie								
Meetkunde	8	8	9	8				
Beschrijvende Meetkunde								
Mechanica								
Natuurkunde	8	9	8	9				
Scheikunde								
Plant- en Dierkunde	9	9	9	9				
Cosmographie								
Geschiedenis	8	7	8	8				
Staatsinrichting								
Staathuishoudkunde								
Aardrijkskunde	8	7	9	8				
Nederlands	8	9	8	8				
Frans	5	7	8	7				
Hoogduits	9	8	9	9				
Engels	7	8	9	8				
Handelswetenschappen	8	9	9	9				
Handtekenen	6	6	6	6				
Rechtlijnig tekenen								
Lichamelijke oefening	8	8	7	7				
Handwerken	9	8	7	8				Z.O.Z.

Gezien: *O. Frank*   Gezien: *O. Frank*   Gezien: *O. Frank*   Gezien:

The 1941–1942 school year had come to an end. As usual, Margot had a glowing report card. This photograph shows Margot's report card from the previous year. Anne's report card was also excellent, except for one poor grade in algebra. But as Anne wrote, *My parents are quite different from most, they don't care a bit whether my reports are good or bad as long as I am well and happy, and not too cheeky, then the rest will come by itself.*

In reality, Anne and Margot's parents were extremely worried about what the future held for them and other Jews in the Netherlands.

"Dear Kitty"

This is possibly the last photograph taken of Anne Frank. In 1942, Jews were forbidden to take pictures, though photographs could be taken of them. No photographs were taken in the years the Frank family spent in hiding—they all had other things on their minds. The photographs which appear in this chapter were taken either before that period or after the war.

Anne was given her diary on her thirteenth birthday, June 12, 1942. Two days later, she began writing in it about her family, her friends, and her school. That June she had a new friend to write about: Hello Silberberg. He was sixteen and Anne thought he was very handsome. Anne was enjoying life and preferred not to dwell on the war. But such thoughtlessness was dangerous for Jews now, as an incident on Monday, June 29, made clear. Toward the end of that afternoon, Hello came to visit Anne at home and meet her parents.

Dear Kitty,

. . . I had bought a cream cake, sweets, and tea and fancy biscuits, quite a spread, but neither Hello nor I felt like sitting stiffly side by side indefinitely, so we went for a walk and it was already ten past eight when he brought me home. Daddy was very cross, and thought it was very wrong of me, and I had to promise to be in by ten to eight in future. (July 1, 1942)

Anne's father was often at home during the day, which Anne thought must be very difficult for him. He must have felt useless without his job. That week at the beginning of July, Anne and her father had a serious talk.

When we walked across our little square together a few days ago Daddy began to talk of us going into hiding, he is very worried that it will be very difficult for us to live completely cut off from the world. I asked him why on earth he was beginning to talk of that already. "Yes, Anne," he said, "you know that we have been taking food, clothes, furniture to other people for more than a year now." (July 5, 1942)

It's an odd idea for someone like me to keep a diary; not only because I have never done so before, but because it seems to me that neither I—nor for that matter anyone else—will be interested in the unbosomings of a thirteen-year-old schoolgirl. (June 20, 1942)

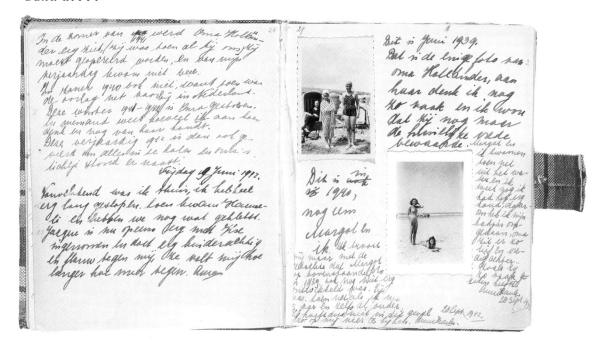

"We don't want our belongings to be seized by the Germans but we certainly don't want to fall into their clutches ourselves. So we shall disappear of our own accord and not wait until they come and fetch us."

"But Daddy, when would it be?"

He spoke so seriously that I grew very anxious.

"Don't you worry about it, we shall arrange everything. Make the most of your carefree young life while you can." (July 5, 1942)

That is all Otto Frank said. Anne just hoped it would never happen!

Anne wrote these words in her diary on Sunday morning, July 5, 1942. But things started to go wrong that very afternoon.

It was a swelteringly hot summer's day. The bell rang at three o'clock. Anne did not hear it because she was relaxing outside on the flat roof,

Anne also stuck photographs in her diary and wrote comments next to them. She wrote this page on Friday, June 19, 1942. On September 28, 1942, she added a few words. Later she stuck some loose sheets in her diary whenever she wanted to add anything.

**Anne on the flat roof of their house
on Merwedeplein in 1940.**

lying back in a chair reading. A little after three,
a very agitated Margot came up to Anne.

*"The S.S. have sent a call-up notice for Daddy," she
whispered. . . . It was a great shock to me, a call-up;
everyone knows what that means. I picture concentration camps and lonely cells—should we let him be
doomed to this? "Of course he won't go," declared Margot while we waited together. "Mummy has gone to the*

v.P.s to ask whether we should move into our hiding place tomorrow. The v.P.s are going with us, there will be 7 of us in all.'' (July 8, 1942)

Both frightened and shocked, Anne and Margot had gone to their bedroom, where Margot suddenly told Anne that the summons was not for their father, but for herself!

I was more frightened than ever and began to cry. Margot is 16, would they really take girls of that age away alone? (July 8, 1942)

But fortunately she would not have to go. The Frank family was going into hiding.

Into hiding . . . but when, how, and where? These were the questions which Anne asked herself over and over.

Anne started to pack her satchel. First her diary went in, then her curlers, handkerchiefs, schoolbooks, comb, and a few letters. *I put in the craziest things with the idea that we were going into hiding, but I'm not sorry, memories mean more to me than dresses.* (July 8, 1942)

Otto Frank knew he could trust Miep Gies and had told her several weeks before his talk with Anne about the plans to go into hiding. He thought very carefully about asking Miep whether she would help his family carry out their plans. She said that of course she would, although she knew how very dangerous it would be.

The evening before the Frank family were to leave their home, Otto wrote this postcard to his sister, Leni Elias-Frank, in Switzerland, hinting that they were going into hiding: "It is a pity that we can no longer correspond with you, but that is how it is. You must understand." Edith, Margot, and Anne also sent their regards. Anne wrote: "I cannot write a letter about the holidays now. Regards and kisses from Anne."

Miep Gies was fetched at the end of the afternoon. Miep came and took away some shoes, dresses, coats, underclothes, and stockings. She returned at eleven o'clock that evening with her husband, Jan, and again left with a lot more of the Franks' possessions. Anne wrote: *I was dog-tired and although I knew it would be my last night in my own bed, I fell asleep immediately.* (July 8, 1942)

Anne was awakened by her mother on Monday morning, July 6, at half past five. It was time to leave.

Anne used two types of handwriting in her diary, printing and cursive. The cursive writing on this page next to her photograph says: *I started with Margot's photograph and finish with my own. This is January 1942. This photograph is horrible, and I look absolutely nothing like it.*

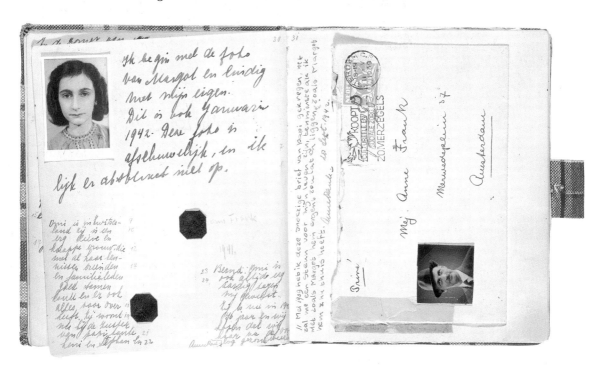

We put on heaps of clothes as if we were going to the North Pole, the sole reason being to take clothes with us. No Jew in our situation would have dreamed of going out with a suitcase full of clothing. I had on two vests, three pairs of pants, a dress on top of that, a skirt, jacket, summer shorts, two pairs of stockings, lace-up shoes, woolly cap, scarf, and still much more; I was nearly stifled before we started, but no one inquired about that. (July 8, 1942)

Miep Gies came to fetch Margot. Margot filled her satchel with schoolbooks, took her bicycle from the bicycle rack, and rode after Miep, a big risk, since Jews were forbidden bicycles. But where were they going? Anne still did not know where the mysterious hiding place was.

The Frank family left their house on Merwedeplein very early on the morning of July 6, 1942. In departing their home of more than eight years, the family left most of their possessions behind. Their cat, Moortje, also had to remain. Anne wrote: *No one knows how often I think of her; whenever I think of her I get tears in my eyes.* **(July 12, 1942)**

Deportation of the Dutch Jews

Jews waiting for transport.

On Monday, June 29, 1942, every Dutch newspaper ran an announcement that the German occupiers had decided to deport all Jews to labor camps in Germany. The Jews in the Netherlands panicked: what would happen to them? What could they do? If they stayed home, they would be caught eventually, as the Germans had already recorded every Jew's name and address. Many Jews thought about going into hiding, but this was an enormously difficult undertaking.

On Sunday, July 5, a thousand Dutch Jews received a card commanding them to report to a given address. Margot Frank was one of this first group. Upon reporting to the address, each Jew was given a form stating when his or her train was leaving and what he or she had to take along. They were told only that the trains were taking them to the camp at Westerbork. No one knew what would happen to them after they arrived.

Over the next year and a half, the Germans called up all the Jews in the Netherlands for deportation. Many did not turn up, so the German police adopted tougher tactics. Without warning, they showed up at a house and took all the Jews away with them. They carried out raids on whole neighborhoods, sometimes with the help of the army, sealing off the area and rounding up all the Jews. People were dragged from their homes, loaded onto trucks, and transferred to the trains that would take them to Westerbork.

The Germans were helped to a large extent by the Dutch police, as well as by Dutch Nazis. When they entered Jewish homes, often the first thing they did was to steal everything of value: money, jewelry, and food. By the end of September 1943, the Germans had succeeded in rounding up nearly all the Jews in the Netherlands. Then they adopted even harsher tactics to uncover and deport the Jews in hiding.

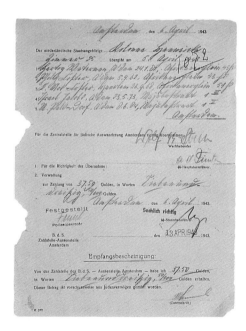

Bounty hunters were used to track down Jews—men, women, and children—who didn't show up for deportation. This is a receipt for 37.50 florins, the reward for betraying five Jews to the German police. This bounty equaled a Dutch average weekly salary.

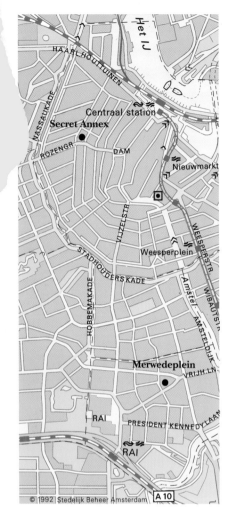

Jews were not permitted to use the tram, the bus, or a car. So Anne and her parents (Margot having left earlier with Miep) walked from Merwedeplein to the Secret Annex on the Prinsengracht Canal, a distance of about two and a half miles. Anne wrote of their journey: *We got sympathetic looks from people on their way to work. You could see by their faces how sorry they were they couldn't offer us a lift, the gaudy yellow star spoke for itself.* (July 9, 1942)

At half past seven Anne and her parents also left the house, closing the door behind them. The only goodbye Anne gave was to Moortje, the cat. The Frank family left a letter to the neighbors asking them to care for Moortje. The house was left in total disarray: breakfast dishes still on the table, the beds unmade. Everything gave the impression that the family had left in a state of panic, but they didn't care about this. *We only wanted to get away, only escape and arrive safely, nothing else.* (July 8, 1942)

Anne described in her diary what happened next, how they left their house and walked through the pouring rain, father, mother, and Anne, each with a school satchel and a shopping bag stuffed full, everything in a jumble. They carried their bags all the way to the hiding place, as Jews were not allowed to use public transportation.

It was only when they were out in the street that her father and mother gradually told Anne the whole plan for going into hiding. For months they had moved all sorts of things from their home to the secret address. They had not planned to go into hiding until July 16, but the

One of the last photographs of Margot. Since Margot was the elder daughter, her parents had told her about their plans for going into hiding before they told Anne. Like Anne, Margot kept a diary during their time in hiding, but it was lost.

The facade of Otto Frank's offices, number 263 Prinsengracht. The warehouse (1) was on the ground floor. The door farthest to the left (2), led to the storage space on the third and fourth floors. The door next to it (3) led to the office on the second floor.

There is another door at the top of the stairs with a frosted glass window in it, which has "Office" written in black letters across it. This is the large main office, very big, very light, and very full. Bep, Miep and Mr. Kleiman work there in the daytime. (July 9, 1942)

Behind this office was a smaller office where Mr. Van Pels used to work with Victor Kugler. Now Victor Kugler worked there alone. The two top floors were used as storage space. Behind this house was another house, not visible from the road, which was connected to number 263 Prinsengracht by a small corridor. This was the Secret Annex.

summons for Margot had pushed the plan forward.

Anne's father told her that the hiding place was in his office. Only Victor Kugler, Johannes Kleiman, Miep Gies, and Bep Voskuijl knew they were coming. Bep's father, Mr. Voskuijl, who worked in the store, didn't find out about it until several weeks later.

When they arrived at the house on the Prinsengracht, Miep quickly took the Frank family upstairs into the Secret Annex. Then Miep left, shutting the door behind her. Margot was already there waiting for her family.

Anne looked around her. There were boxes and piles of bedding everywhere. It was an indescribable mess. They immediately set to work.

The whole day long we unpacked boxes, filled cupboards, hammered and tidied, until we were dead beat. We sank into clean beds that night. (July 10, 1942)

This is the ground-floor warehouse, where the spices were ground, weighed, and packed. Of the three men who worked here, only Bep Voskuijl's father knew about the family in hiding behind the office.

The next morning they picked up where they had left off. With all the cleaning and organizing to do, Anne hardly had any time to think about the great changes in her life. It was not until the following day, Wednesday, that she could write the details of this momentous event in her diary.

Then I had a chance, for the first time since our arrival, to tell you all about it, and at the same time to realize myself what had happened to me, and what was still going to happen. (July 10, 1942)

This photograph was taken just after the war. The Secret Annex is highlighted in yellow, the house at the front in red. Here you can see the small window in the attic that provided Anne with a view of the Westertoren, the large clock tower on the right. Another attic window at the back of the Annex looked out onto a courtyard with a large chestnut tree (in green), which Anne wrote about several times in her diary.

This is the Secret Annex as seen from the rear courtyard garden. The branches of the chestnut tree are on the right.

1. Anne's room, which she first shared with Margot and later with Fritz Pfeffer.
2. Otto and Edith Frank's room. Later Margot joined them.
3. The room of Mr. and Mrs. Van Pels. The families also cooked and ate together in this room.
4. The food supplies were stored in the attic. Later it became Anne's favorite place to sit quietly and gaze out of the window.
5. Otto Frank's old private office. It was not part of the hiding place, but was used by the staff at number 263 Prinsengracht.
6. The kitchen. This also was only used by the office staff.

Over the next few days, Anne explored every inch of the hiding place.

The family was terrified of being discovered. During the daytime they had to walk quietly and talk softly so that the people in the store would not hear them. They also had to be very cautious about being heard or spotted by the neighbors.

We made curtains straight away on the first day, really one can hardly call them curtains they are only loose drafty strips of material, all different shapes, quality and pattern, which Daddy and I sewed together in a most unprofessional way; these works of art are fixed in position with drawing pins not to come down until we emerge from here. (July 11, 1942)

Their only contact with the outside world was through Miep Gies, Bep Voskuijl, Victor Kugler,

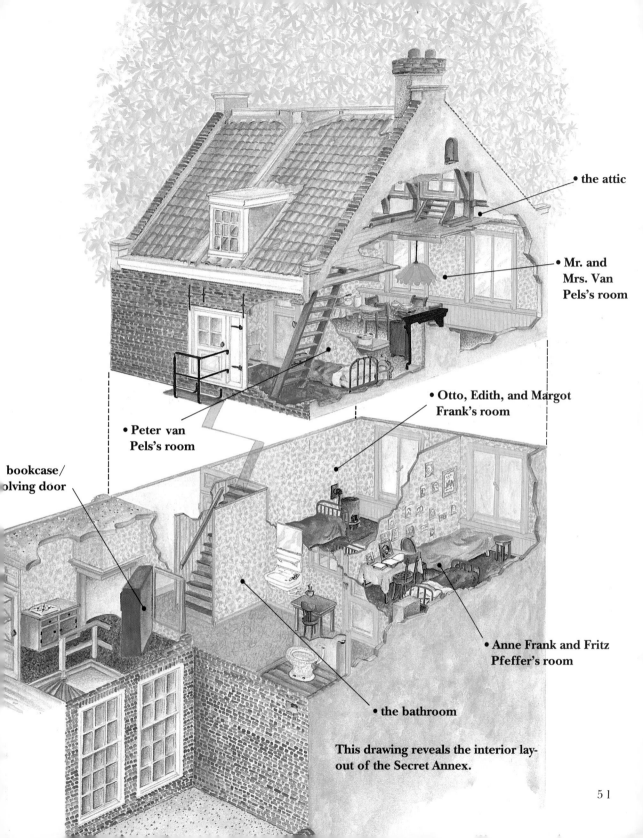

• the attic

• Mr. and Mrs. Van Pels's room

• Otto, Edith, and Margot Frank's room

• Peter van Pels's room

bookcase/ olving door

• Anne Frank and Fritz Pfeffer's room

• the bathroom

This drawing reveals the interior layout of the Secret Annex.

51

Anne and Margot's room. *Our little room looked very bare at first with nothing on the walls; but thanks to Daddy who had brought my picture post-cards and film-star collection on before-hand, and with the aid of paste pot and brush I have transformed the walls into one gigantic picture. This makes it look much more cheerful.* **(July 11, 1942)**

Anne wrote most of her diary at the table in this room. This photograph was taken after the war, when the room was temporarily furnished according to the instructions of Otto Frank and Miep Gies. Now the room stands empty.

and Johannes Kleiman. The four helpers bought food, brought books, and told the Franks what was happening in Amsterdam. The world had become very small for Anne Frank: a few rooms and two attic windows, her only portals to the world outside. She wrote in her diary: *I can't tell you how oppressive it is* never *to be able to go outdoors, also I am very afraid that we will be discovered and shot.* (September 28, 1942)

Anne was very glad when the Van Pels family joined them on July 13, 1942. (In the published version of her diary the Van Pels family is referred to as the Van Daan family.) There were three members of the Van Pels family: Mr. and Mrs. Van Pels and their fifteen-year-old son, Peter. Peter had brought along his cat, Mouschi.

The v.P.s arrived on July 13. We thought they were coming on the 14th, but between 13 and 16 July the Germans called up people right and left which created more and more unrest, so they played for safety, better a day too early than a day too late. (August 14, 1942)

The families' survival in the Secret Annex completely depended upon their helpers, who were all close colleagues of Otto Frank and current office staff. From left to right: Miep Gies, Johannes Kleiman, Otto Frank, Victor Kugler, and Bep Voskuijl.

Going into Hiding

Many people in hiding did not have as spacious rooms as the Frank family. These people are living in secret under the floorboards of a house.

Many Jews tried to escape German deportation by going into hiding, though this had become extremely difficult. Where could they go? When the war began, no organizations existed to help people go underground. Anyone who wanted to go into hiding had to have the help of non-Jews to provide a secret home and all the provisions needed from the outside. But as a result of all the measures introduced by the Germans, most Jews had lost all their non-Jewish friends and acquaintances.

It hardly ever happened that a whole family could hide in one place. The Frank family was remarkably lucky. It was easier to find a place for children to hide than for adults, since a child could easily be passed off as a cousin from the city. Some parents, in order to save their children, gave them to complete strangers.

Finding a place to hide was difficult enough. Finding enough money to do it could be even harder. Often people demanded that the Jews pay a lot of money for their keep, something most Jews could not afford, especially after the Germans had deprived them of their jobs and incomes.

Going into hiding held many dangers. Anyone caught would be sent to a concentration camp. The punishment for a non-Jew helping Jews was equally severe. For this reason alone, many Jews decided against going underground. Fortunately, there were still many people who helped the Jews, despite the dangers.

Several thousand Jewish children were saved. Many found a place to hide with farmers in the countryside. Most of them never saw their parents again.

These helpers were usually the Jews' only contact with the outside world. They provided food, brought newspapers and books, and tried to find a doctor who could be trusted when anyone fell ill. Equally important, they provided encouragement and reassurance to their secret charges. Helping the Jews was a heavy responsibility, full of risks. Many helpers suffered the full measure of those risks when they were captured by the Germans and sent to the concentration camps.

It was not until the summer of 1943 that a secret organization was set up to help people in hiding. But by this time, the great majority of Jews had already been deported. As the war went on, more and more non-Jews went into hiding: people who refused to join the forced-labor squads sent to Germany, members of the Resistance who were wanted by the authorities. An estimated 250,000 to 300,000 people were in hiding for some period during the war in the Netherlands alone.

Of the 140,000 Jews in the Netherlands, about 25,000 eventually went into hiding. Of these, it is estimated that 16,000 survived the war. The remaining 9,000 were discovered and deported. Often they had been betrayed.

Once the Van Pelses had moved in, life for Anne held more fun and a bit less quiet. The quiet had made her rather nervous.

Days passed, turned into weeks and then months. During the daytime when the staff of the office was working, the Franks and Van Pelses could only whisper and had to walk around very softly in their stocking feet. No one in the Secret Annex was allowed to use a faucet or toilet between the office hours of nine o'clock in the morning and seven o'clock in the evening.

We are as quiet as baby mice. Who, 3 months ago, would have guessed that quicksilver Anne would have to sit still for hours—and what's more, could? (October 1, 1942)

The room of Mr. and Mrs. Van Pels.

If you go up the next flight of stairs and open the door, you are simply amazed that there could be such a big light room in such an old house by the canal. There is a stove in this room . . . and a sink. This is now the kitchen as well as bedroom for the v.P. couple, besides being general living room, dining room, and scullery. (July 9, 1942)

The trash was burned in the stove. This was done only after dark during the summer, as seeing the smoke rising from the chimney might have made a neighbor suspicious.

This room was also temporarily furnished for the photograph as directed by Otto Frank and Miep Gies. The room is now empty.

Peter van Pels. Anne described Peter's arrival in the Secret Annex as follows: *At nine-thirty in the morning (we were still having breakfast) Peter arrived, the v.P.s' son, not sixteen yet, rather soft, shy, gawky youth; can't expect much from his company.* (August 14, 1942)

What did Anne do during those long daytime hours? She spent a lot of time studying her schoolbooks, a large pile of which had been taken along. She also read many books which Miep brought her, and learned shorthand. Margot and Peter also spent many hours on their schoolwork every day. Otto Frank helped all three children and tested them on their lessons. None of them wanted to fall behind in their studies. They still hoped that they would be able to return to school soon.

Many Jews in the Netherlands were picked up during these months and taken to concentration camps. Though the Frank and Van Pels families had escaped this, they could not escape being crowded on top of each other day and night. They saw and heard everything everyone did. This lack of privacy, as well as the never-ending fear of discovery, put everyone constantly on edge. It is therefore not surprising that arguments were a regular part of life in the Annex.

Anne wrote: *Why do grownups quarrel so easily, so much, and over the most idiotic things? Up till now I thought that only children squabbled.* (September 28, 1942)

Hermann and Auguste van Pels. Mr. Van Pels had been Otto Frank's partner at the Prinsengracht office for several years. Until 1942, the families had little contact, so Anne didn't know any of the Van Pelses well.

Anne, too, found her new life difficult. She had lost everything: her friends, her school, her freedom. Sometimes she rebelled, and sometimes sadness overtook her and she often cried at night. But during the day she was different: lively and boisterous, and usually surprisingly cheerful. She had something to say about everything and everyone, and was always ready with a quick answer. Mr. and Mrs. Van Pels thought her behavior insolent and believed she had been brought up badly. Edith Frank regularly argued with Anne, and Margot was often short-tempered with her. Peter wasn't much help, either.

When the Frank family moved into the Secret Annex on July 6, this bookcase had not yet been built, and a single door led to the Annex rooms. Anne wrote: *No one would ever guess that there would be so many rooms hidden behind that plain door painted gray. There's a little step in front of the door and then you are inside.* (July 9, 1942).

For safety's sake, it was necessary to hide this entrance. Over a month later Anne wrote in her diary:

Dear Kitty,
The entrance to our hiding place has now been properly concealed. Mr. Kugler thought it would be better to put a cupboard in front of our door . . . but of course it had to be a movable cupboard that can open like a door. Mr. Voskuijl made the whole thing. . . . (We had already let Mr. Voskuijl into the secret and he can't do enough to help.) If we want to go downstairs we have to first bend down and then jump. The first 3 days we were all going about with masses of lumps on our foreheads because we all knocked ourselves against the low doorway. So Peter has made it as soft as possible by nailing a cloth filled with wood wool against the top of the door. Let's see if that helps!
(August 21, 1942)

Margot and Peter aren't a bit what you would call "young," they are both so staid and quiet. I show up terribly against them and am always hearing "You don't find Margot and Peter doing that—why don't you just once follow your dear sister's example?" I simply loathe it. (February 5, 1943)

Anne felt truly alone and misunderstood. Her diary had become her one really good friend.

Most of the time life in the Annex was simply boring. Yet there were also moments of great excitement—and great fear. One evening at eight o'clock the bell suddenly rang loudly. Everyone was terrified. Was it the German police, the Gestapo? Was it the end? They all held their breaths. But there was no more noise.

Three weeks later, a more frightening experience occurred.

Miep and Jan Gies celebrated their first wedding anniversary on July 16, 1942, ten days after the Franks went into hiding. On July 18, the family prepared a festive meal in the Secret Annex with the food that Miep had bought. This is the menu Anne typed for the occasion, which she humorously composed as if it described a formal dinner in a fancy French restaurant. A potato was called "Pomme de terre" and gravy was called "sauce de boeuf," which Anne suggested the guests should "please use minimally because of the reduction of the butter rations." The meal was capped by "Coffee with sugar, cream and several surprises."

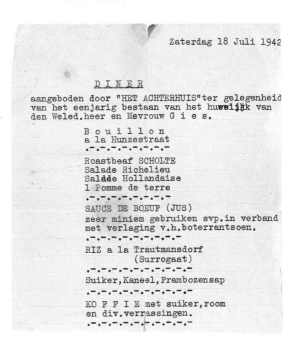

Victor Kugler (right) and Johannes Kleiman (left) helped the families in hiding whenever they could. Like Miep and Bep, they often visited them in the Secret Annex during the lunch hour when the staff in the warehouse had gone home. They talked about the practical problems of being in hiding, but they also talked about the political situation and the way things were going with the business.

From the landing opposite the bookcase came the sound of hammering. All talk inside the Annex immediately ceased. A quarter of an hour later, someone knocked on the bookcase door. Everyone turned pale. The knocking continued and they could hear someone pulling and pushing at the door.

Just as I thought my last hour was at hand, we heard Mr. Kleiman's voice say "open the door, it's only me." (October 20, 1942)

Then they learned what had happened. Johannes Kleiman explained that a carpenter was in the house to check the fire extinguishers, and that he had not had time to warn them. The carpenter had gone downstairs again. It was a great relief.

On Tuesday, November 10, 1942, Anne heard that an eighth person was coming to hide with them. *We have always thought that there was quite enough room and food for one more. We were only afraid of giving Kugler and Kleiman more trouble. But now that the appalling stories we hear about Jews are getting even worse Daddy got hold of two agents who had to decide and they thought it was an excellent plan. It is just as dangerous for 7 as for 8 they said, and quite rightly.* (November 10, 1942)

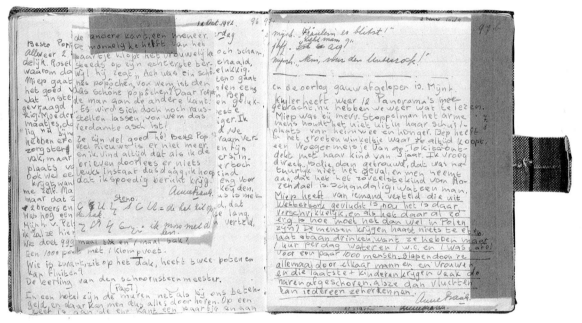

Anne started on a written course of shorthand. *Bep has written to some secretarial school or other and ordered a correspondence course in shorthand for Margot, Peter and me. You wait and see what perfect experts we shall be by next year. In any case it's extremely important to be able to write in a code.*
(October 1, 1942)

Six months later, Anne wrote: *We have finished our Shorthand course; now we are beginning to practice speed, aren't we getting clever?* **(March 27, 1943)**

They chose someone they knew, and who they thought would fit in well: Fritz Pfeffer. (In the published version of her diary, he was called Albert Dussel.)

Fritz Pfeffer arrived a week later. He was amazed to find the Franks. Like the family's neighbors, friends, and acquaintances, he had believed that the Franks had fled abroad.

Anne liked him, and listened to what he had to say about the outside world. It made everyone feel very somber. *Countless friends and acquaintances have gone to a terrible end. Evening after evening the green and gray army lorries trundle past and ring at every front door to inquire if there are any Jews living in the house, if there are, then the whole family has to go at once. If they don't find any they go on to the next house. No one has a chance of evading them, unless one goes into hiding. . . . Nobody is spared, old people, children, babies, expectant mothers, the sick each and all join in the march of death.* (November 19, 1942)

Fritz Pfeffer fled to the Netherlands in 1938. The Frank family had known him for a few years. Anne had to share her room with him, and Margot went to sleep in her parents' bedroom.

This was the living room and bedroom of Otto and Edith Frank. The door on the right opened into Anne's room. When the room was occupied, curtains would have been kept drawn over the windows. When Fritz Pfeffer came, Margot also slept in this room, on a camp bed which was set up every night. The photograph was taken after the war. This room is also empty now.

This made Anne realize how lucky she was in the Secret Annex. She thought about her dearest friends, now far away, all *delivered into the hands of the cruelest brutes the world has ever seen,* and she lamented: *And all because they are Jews.* (November 19, 1942)

The days and weeks crawled by. Autumn passed into winter. It was cold and dark very early. After four o'clock or half past four, it was too dark to read. *We pass the time in all sorts of crazy ways: asking riddles, physical training in the dark, talking English and French, criticizing books, but it all begins to pall in the end.* (November 28, 1942)

The families in hiding had now been living on top of each other for nearly six months, always with the fear of being discovered. They could never go outside, not even for a moment.

On October 18, 1942, Anne stuck a photograph of herself in her diary and wrote next to it: *This is a photograph of me as I wish I looked all the time. Then I might still have a chance of getting to Hollywood. But at present, I'm afraid, I usually look quite different.*

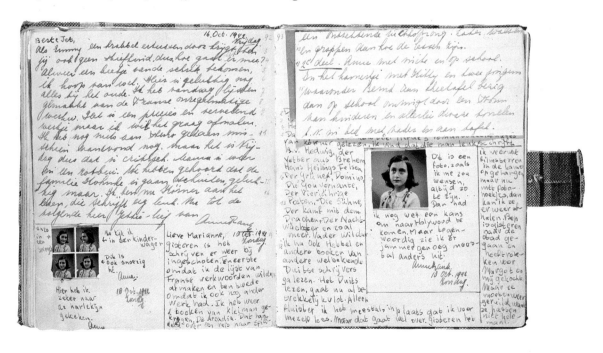

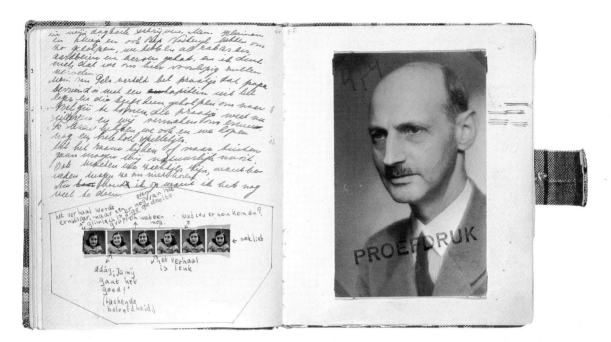

Anne's view of Fritz Pfeffer quickly changed. *Now he shows himself in his true colors; a stodgy, old-fashioned disciplinarian and preacher of long, drawn-out sermons on manners. As I have the unusual good fortune (!) to share my bedroom, alas, a small one, with his lordship and as I am generally considered to be the most badly behaved of the three young people, I have a lot to put up with and have to sham deafness in order to escape the much too often repeated tickings-off and warnings.* (November 28, 1942)

Nevertheless, such criticism of herself did not leave her unaffected. Anne's lack of concern was only pretend. In reality, she wanted to improve herself, and often berated herself when she could not. *Now the trying part about me is that I scold myself more and am much harder on myself than anyone else; then if Mummy adds her share of advice the pile of*

Anne stuck this photograph of Otto Frank in her diary. Anne was very attached to her father. Otto defended her when the others criticized her, consoled her when she was sad, and helped her with her studies. He was her support and refuge. Otto understood how difficult it must be for the lively, active Anne to live in hiding, always having to whisper and sit still during the day, never able to go outside. He tried to help her whenever he could. Anne wrote: *I adore Daddy, he is the one I look up to. I don't love anyone in the world but him.* (November 7, 1942)

Stores of food were kept in the attic of the Secret Annex. Sometimes the helpers succeeded in getting hold of large stocks of canned goods or beans on the black market. Miep and Bep went shopping every day, buying what they could with coupons, which had been distributed by the government when certain foods became scarce and had to be rationed. During the families' time in hiding, finding enough food for them became increasingly difficult. The Netherlands was enduring a food shortage, since a great many goods were being shipped out to Germany.

On March 14, 1944, Anne wrote: *Our food coupon suppliers have been caught so we just have our 5 black-market ration cards and no coupons and no fats. . . . Our supper today consists of a hash made from kale which has been preserved in a barrel. . . . It's incredible how kale that is probably a few years old can stink! The smell in the room is a mixture of bad plums, strong preservatives and 10 rotten eggs. Ugh! The mere thought of eating that muck makes me feel sick!* **(March 14, 1944)**

sermons becomes so insurmountable that in my despair I become rude and start contradicting. (June 13, 1944)

The new year 1943 arrived.

Every night the families heard hundreds of Allied airplanes flying over, heading toward bombing raids on German towns. This gave them hope. The opposition to Germany was getting stronger. Every evening they listened tensely to the Dutch radio program broadcast from England for news about the war.

And every evening they listened to the German antiaircraft guns shooting at the Allied planes.

I still haven't got over my fear of everything connected with shooting and planes, and I creep into Daddy's bed nearly every night for comfort. I know it's very childish but you don't know what it is like, the A.A. guns roar so loudly that you can't hear yourself speak. (March 10, 1943)

Mrs. Van Pels was also very scared, but not only of the guns. One night she thought she heard a burglar in the attic, where the food was stored. No one took her seriously, but a few days later the noise woke the whole Van Pels family.

Peter went up to the attic with a torch [flashlight] *and scamper, scamper, what do you think was running away? A swarm of enormous rats!*

When we knew who the thieves were we let Mouschi sleep in the attic and the uninvited guests didn't come back again, at least . . . not during the night. (March 10, 1943)

A few days later Peter went up to the attic to fetch some old newspapers. To get down the steps he had to hold the trapdoor firmly. Without looking, he put down his hand and . . . almost fell down the steps with shock and pain. Without

Once the helpers were able to buy several bags of brown beans. Peter was asked to take the bags up to the attic. *He had managed to get 5 of the 6 sacks upstairs intact, and he was just busy pulling up number 6, when the bottom seam of the sack split and a shower—no a positive hailstorm of brown beans came pouring down and rattled down the stairs. There were about fifty pounds in the sack and the noise was enough to waken the dead. Downstairs they thought the old house with all its contents was coming down on them. It gave Peter a moment's fright, but he was soon roaring with laughter, especially when he saw me standing at the bottom of the stairs like a little island in the middle of a sea of beans! I was entirely surrounded up to my ankles in beans.* (November 9, 1942)

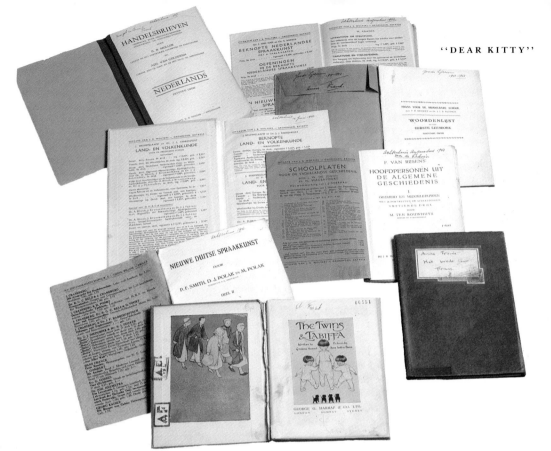

Schoolbooks. Every day Margot, Anne, and Peter spent a few hours on their school subjects: languages, algebra, geometry, geography, and history. They all hoped that the war would be over soon, and that they would be able to go back to school. Otto Frank was the one who helped them with their schoolwork. Anne wrote about it several times:

I have a great loathing for Algebra, Geometry and figures. I enjoy all the other school subjects, but history above all! **(April 6, 1944) Later she wrote of her math book:** *I've never loathed any other book so much as that one. . . . If I'm ever in a really very wicked mood I'll tear the blasted thing to pieces!* **(May 20, 1944)**

knowing it, he had put his hand on a large rat, which bit his arm savagely. By the time he'd made it down the stairs, the blood had soaked through his pajamas, his knees were shaking, and he was as white as a sheet. Anne could well imagine what it was like: *And no wonder; it's not very pleasant to stroke a large rat; and to get bitten into the bargain is really dreadful.* (March 10, 1943)

Anne enjoyed writing very much and didn't confine herself to her diary. In 1943, she also started writing a book titled "Stories and Events from the Secret Annex." This book included descriptions of happenings in the Secret Annex and memories from Anne's schooldays, as well as fairy tales and other imaginary tales, which she called "Made-up Stories."

The thing you notice right away about the storybook is its neatness. Anne wrote page after page in fine script with her fountain pen, hardly ever crossing anything out or making a mistake. The chapters were carefully divided, much as they are in a real book. By way of introduction to the story "Paula's Flight," Anne wrote: *Long ago, when I was little, Papa used to tell me stories about "naughty Paula", he had a whole collection of stories and I was crazy about them. And now again, when I'm with Papa at night, he sometimes tells me about Paula, and I've written down the latest story.*
(December 22, 1943)

Daily Life

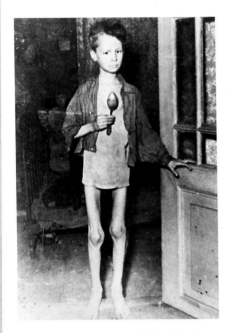

In the winter of 1944–45, thousands of people died of hunger and cold in the western Netherlands.

At the beginning of the war, most people tried not to become involved with anything connected to it. However, it soon became impossible not to get involved. Chocolate, coffee, cigarettes, and many other once common items became luxuries virtually impossible to buy. People had to surrender their bicycles and radios. Anything of value was taken to Germany by the occupying forces. More and more people were entering the ranks of the very poor.

The official newspapers contained only articles approved by the Germans, ones that said the German Army was winning battles everywhere, that members of the Resistance were all criminals, and that Jews were an inferior race.

But more and more underground newspapers appeared, papers that had to be written and printed in secret because they told the truth about German losses. People also secretly listened to *Radio Oranje*, a program in Dutch broadcast every night from London. Oranje is the name of the Dutch Royal Family.

In 1943, it became clear that Germany would lose the war. Increasing numbers of people began complaining openly about the occupation. The Resistance gained strength, though the German occupying forces tried to suppress it. Members of the Resistance were often simply shot dead in the street, a method the Germans used to intimidate the people who might sympathize with Resistance workers.

In the autumn of 1944, the Allies liberated the south of the Netherlands. The rest of the country remained occupied. That winter there was a severe food shortage in the western Netherlands, particularly in the big cities, where there was hardly any food left. About 20,000 people died that winter from hunger, cold, and disease.

On May 5, 1945, the whole of the Netherlands was liberated after five years of war.

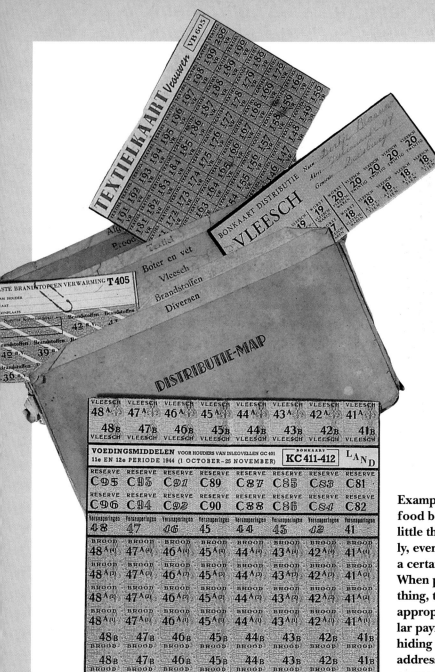

Examples of coupons issued when food became scarce. So that what little there was could be shared fairly, every registered citizen received a certain number of coupons. When people wished to buy something, they had to surrender the appropriate coupon as well as regular payment. People who were in hiding did not have an official address, so couldn't receive coupons. They and their helpers had to rely on coupon suppliers in the Resistance to purchase scarce items.

Sometimes when there was no one in the office, they would leave their hiding place for a while. When it was dark, Anne would look out of the office window at the front of the house. From behind the curtain, she would see people passing by and catch a glimpse of the outside world. Of course, they all made very sure that they would not be seen.

Spring 1943. The eight people in the Annex were all tense and tired. Everyone was suffering from lack of sleep because of the sounds of airplanes and antiaircraft fire. The food they had was poor. There were shortages of everything. Miep and Bep had more and more trouble finding food for them. Anne greatly admired the Dutch people who were helping those in hiding, for it was difficult and dangerous work. *It is amazing how much noble, unselfish work these people are doing, risking their own lives to help and save others. Our helpers are a very good example. . . . Never have we heard* one *word of the burden which we certainly must be to them, never has one of them complained about all the trouble we cause.* (January 28, 1944)

Anne often realized that she should not complain. *If I just think of how we live here, I usually come to the conclusion that it is a paradise compared with how other Jews who are not in hiding must be living.* (May 2, 1943)

On Friday morning, July 16, 1943, the people in hiding were shocked by the discovery that a burglar had been in the warehouse. Both the door of the warehouse and the front door were open, having been forced with a crowbar. Johannes Kleiman, who arrived at the office shortly after this discovery, found that two cashboxes had been stolen. But worst of all, the thieves had also taken coupons for 150 kilos (over 330 pounds) of sugar. Everyone was scared that the burglars had noticed there was someone hiding upstairs and would betray them to the police.

But fortunately, as the days went by, nothing happened.

The people in the Annex tried to live as normally as possible, following a fixed schedule every day. But the days were so tedious. Would the war go on much longer? How long could they all keep it up? These were the questions they all asked themselves.

Then on September 8, 1943, they found new hope for a happy ending. On the radio they heard

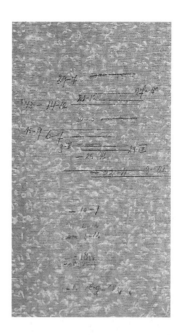

Anne was just thirteen when she went into hiding. She was growing visibly. On the wall in Otto and Edith Frank's room, just next to the door to Anne's room, they kept a record of Anne's and Margot's heights. The stripes on the wall show that during her time in the Secret Annex, Anne grew a full thirteen centimeters (over five inches), a rapid spurt that was not without problems. All the clothes which Anne had brought with her in July 1942 soon became much too small for her. Sometimes Miep or Bep would bring her something new. *Mummy and Margot have managed the whole winter with 3 vests between them, and mine are so small that they don't even come to my tummy.* (May 2, 1943)

By this time, the diary which Anne had received for her thirteenth birthday in 1942 had been long since filled up. She continued her diary entries in the exercise and accounting books which Miep and Bep had given her. In January 1944, Anne reread her "old" diary, and realized that in the previous year and a half she had changed a great deal. She thought she had "grown wiser." When she noticed that there were still two empty pages, she wrote down her thoughts about what she had read.

When I look over my diary today, 1 1/2 years on, I cannot believe that I was ever such an innocent young thing. . . . I still understand those moods, those remarks about Margot, Mummy and Daddy so well that I might have written them yesterday, but I no longer understand how I could write so freely about other things. (January 22, 1944)

that Italy, an ally of Germany, had surrendered to the Allies. Would the war end in 1943 after all?

But events did not move that fast, and the Allied invasion of Europe, which they hoped for every day, did not take place. In the autumn of 1943, Anne was frequently in a very gloomy mood. *My nerves often get the better of me: it is especially on Sundays that I feel rotten. The atmosphere is so oppressive, and sleepy and as heavy as lead; you don't hear a single bird singing outside, and a deadly sultry silence hangs everywhere, catching hold of me as if it would drag me down deep into an underworld. . . . "Go outside, laugh, and take a breath of fresh air," a voice cries within me; but I don't even feel a response any more; I go and lie on the divan and sleep, to make the time pass more quickly, and the stillness and the terrible fear, because there is no way of killing time.* (October 29, 1943)

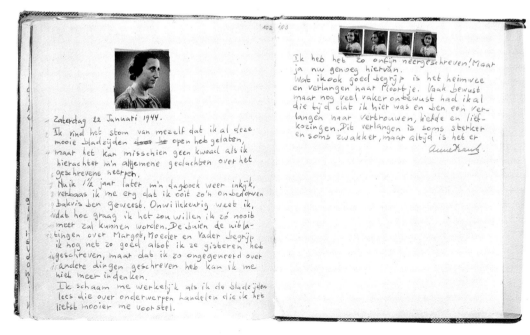

Wednesday, 23 February 1944
Dear Kitty,
*   It's lovely weather again and I've quite perked up since yesterday. . . . This morning when I went to the attic again, Peter was busy clearing up. He was finished very quickly and when I sat down on my favorite spot on the floor, he joined me. Both of us looked at the glorious blue of the sky, the bare chestnut tree on whose branches little raindrops shone, at the seagulls and other birds that looked like silver in the sun. . . . He stood and I sat, we breathed the fresh air, looked outside, and both felt that the spell should not be broken.*

It was 1944. Anne was now more than fourteen and a half years old. The group of eight people had been hiding in the Secret Annex for a year and a half. Anne noticed that her thoughts and feelings were changing, and she wrote about this in her diary. She spent much more time thinking about all sorts of things, and also viewed the people with whom she was hiding in a new light. Anne also noticed that she was changing physically.

I think what is happening to me is so wonderful, and not only what can be seen on my body, but all that is taking place inside. I never discuss myself or any of these things with anybody; that is why I have to talk to myself about them. (January 5, 1944)

Anne was no longer a noisy schoolgirl. She was growing up . . . and falling in love!

The object of this new love was Peter. She wanted to talk to him about everything that was on her mind. But Peter was shy and avoided her. However, Anne found a way of getting him to talk.

I tried to think of an excuse to stay unobtrusively in his room and get him talking, and my chance came yesterday. Peter has a mania for crossword puzzles at the moment . . . we soon sat opposite each other at his little table, he on the chair and me on the divan.

It gave me a queer feeling when I looked into his deep blue eyes and saw how embarrassed this unexpected visit had made him. (January 6, 1944)

On January 12, 1944, Anne wrote about Margot: *Margot has grown so sweet; she seems quite different from what she used to be, isn't nearly so catty these days and is becoming a real friend. Nor does she any longer regard me as a little kid who counts for nothing.*

For a time Anne thought that Margot was also in love with Peter, but that was not the case. However, Margot was a little bit jealous. In a letter to Anne, she wrote: *"I only feel a bit sorry that I haven't found anyone yet, and am not likely to for the time being, with whom I can discuss my thoughts and feelings."* (March 20, 1944)

Anne and Margot wrote letters to each other, as Anne wrote in her diary, *Because I can say what I mean much better on paper.* (March 20, 1944)

Anne was highly critical of her mother, who she thought neither understood her nor took her seriously. They often quarreled, though Anne kept trying to make up with her. On March 2, 1944, Anne described one of these quarrels. Bep was in the Secret Annex helping wash the dishes and talking to Edith Frank and Mrs. Van Pels about feeling discouraged. Anne listened in on the conversation. *Do you know what her advice was? She should try to think of all the other people who are in trouble! What is the good of thinking of misery when one is already miserable oneself? I said this too and was naturally told to keep out of this sort of conversation!* (March 2, 1944)

Anne was furious. *Aren't the grownups idiotic and stupid? . . . I'm not allowed to open my mouth! . . . We aren't even allowed to have any opinions!* (March 2, 1944)

In the following weeks, Anne and Peter became more and more comfortable in each other's company, although Peter was still shy. Anne often went to Peter's room, where they could be alone and talk.

Anne thought a great deal about her past and about what the future held. She thought back to the happy, carefree days before they had gone into hiding and everything had changed. She had changed as well. As soon as she moved into the Annex, she became rebellious and insolent and was constantly reprimanded by the adults around her. Now, a year and a half later, she thought that she had "grown wiser." She was still sometimes cheerful and boisterous, talking back to the

Anne often visited Peter in the attic, visits which simultaneously made her feel happy and sad: *When Peter and I are sitting somewhere together, on a hard, wooden crate in the midst of masses of rubbish and dust, our arms around each other's shoulders, and very close; he with one of my curls in his hand. When the birds sing outside and you see the trees changing to green, the sun invites one to be out in the open air, when the sky is so blue, then—oh, then I wish for so much!* **(April 14, 1944)**

adults whenever she felt like it. But Anne believed that this was only one side of her, the superficial exterior, which was what all other people saw of her. She thought she had changed "inside," becoming more aware of her good and bad qualities and of what was most important to her. She wanted to be happy. She did not want to think about all the misery in the world, but about all the beautiful things that remained. She was greatly troubled by the fact that the adults still frequently treated her like a child. *Although I'm only fourteen, I know quite well what I want, I know who is right and who is wrong, I have my opinions, my own ideas and principles.* (March 17, 1944)

On Saturday evening, March 18, Anne visited Peter again. *He was standing on the left side of the open window; I went and stood on the right side, and we talked. It was much easier to talk beside the open window in semidarkness than in bright light and I believe Peter felt the same. We told each other so much, so very very much, that I can't repeat it all, but it was lovely, the most wonderful evening I have ever had in the "Secret Annex."* (March 19, 1944)

The adults were very curious about what Peter and Anne were discussing upstairs, and they

The warehouse. While the Franks were in hiding, there were at least three burglaries. With everything in increasingly short supply, an epidemic of theft had broken out in Amsterdam. After each burglary, the family feared that the thieves might have noticed something and would betray them. But there was another danger. Two members of the staff who worked in the warehouse had never been told about the hiding place. At least one of them suspected something. He knew there had once been an entrance to a series of rooms in the back, and was curious about why Miep and Bep regularly went upstairs with bags of groceries.

On Wednesday, March 29, 1944, during the daily radio broadcast from London, Anne heard the Dutch minister, Bolkestein, say that after the war all the diaries and letters about the war would be collected. Anne fantasized: *Just imagine how interesting it would be if I were to publish a romance of the "Secret Annex."* (March 29, 1944) She could not forget the idea. A week later she wrote: *Will I ever become a journalist or a writer? I hope so, oh, I hope so very much, for I can recapture everything when I write, my thoughts, my ideals and my fantasies.* (April 5, 1944)

On May 11, 1944, she confided in her diary: *You've known for a long time that my greatest wish is to become a journalist someday and later on a famous writer. . . . In any case, I want to publish a book entitled <u>het Achterhuis</u> (The Secret Annex) after the war, whether I shall succeed or not, I cannot say, but my diary will be a great help.*

made silly jokes about it. But behind the jokes, Anne's parents were worried about their daughter.

On Sunday, April 9, 1944, there was yet another burglary. This was the most frightening thing yet. The front door onto the street had been destroyed, and it seemed that someone had warned the police, who came to search the building. *Then, a quarter past 11, a bustle and noise downstairs. Everyone's breath was audible, in other respects no one moved. Footsteps in the house, in the private office, kitchen, then . . . on our staircase, no one breathed audibly now, 8 hearts thumped, footsteps on our staircase, then a rattling of the swinging cupboard. This moment is indescribable:*

"Now we are lost!" I said and could see all fifteen of us being carried off by the Gestapo that very night. (April 11, 1944)

Twice they rattled the cupboard, then a tin can fell down, the footsteps withdrew, we were saved thus far! A shiver seemed to pass from one to the other, I heard someone's teeth chattering, no one said a word. (April 11, 1944)

They all spent that night together in the Van Pelses' room, though no one slept. They were all too terrified. The next morning they were delighted when the helpers arrived. Once again, everything had turned out right.

April 15, 1944, was an important day in Anne's life, the day of her first kiss. Peter and Anne were sitting close together on the divan in Peter's room. *How I suddenly made the right move, I don't know, but before we went downstairs he kissed me, through my*

hair, half on my left cheek, half on my ear; I tore down-stairs without looking round, and am simply longing for today. (April 16, 1944)

In the days that followed, Anne thought again and again about that first kiss and how things might now be different. In her diary she wrote: *Dear Kitty, Do you think that Daddy and Mummy would approve of my sitting and kissing a boy on a divan—a boy of seventeen and a half and a girl of just under fifteen? I don't really think they would, but I must rely on myself over this. It is so quiet and peaceful to lie in his arms and to dream, it is so thrilling to feel his cheek against mine, it is lovely to know that there is someone waiting for me.* (April 17, 1944)

Anne's original diary and photograph album, and the additional diary volumes and loose sheets. When Anne had filled her first diary, she continued writing in exercise and accounting books. She kept everything in a leather briefcase which had belonged to her father. A few weeks after Anne heard that diaries would be collected after the war, she decided to rewrite her own diary so that it could be published. While copying the diary, she also edited it, adding some things and taking out others. The fresh copy was made on thin sheets of tracing paper which she got from the office. Sometimes she doubted the point of doing all this. On April 14, 1944, she wrote: *I really believe Kits, that I'm slightly bats today, and yet I don't know why. Everything here is so mixed up, nothing's connected any more, and sometimes I very much doubt whether in the future anyone will be interested in all my tosh.*

"The unbosomings of an ugly duckling," will be the title of all this nonsense.

Anne wrote a long letter to her father to explain why she would continue to visit Peter. At the end of it she wrote: *You can't and mustn't regard me as fourteen, for all these troubles have made me older; I shall not be sorry for what I have done but shall act as I think I can!* (May 5, 1944) She asked her father to trust her through thick and thin, but Otto was angry and disappointed with her. Later Anne was sorry about her angry and passionate letter, but not about her feelings for Peter. *I am not alone any more; he loves me. I love him.* (May 7, 1944)

Anne decided to talk to her father about her feelings for Peter. When they were alone one day, she asked: *"Daddy I expect you've gathered that when we are together, Peter and I don't sit miles apart. Do you think it's wrong?"* (May 2, 1944) Her father warned Anne to be careful. The next day he told her that it would be better if she did not go to Peter's room so often. But Anne did not want to obey her father. *Not only because I like being with Peter; but I have told him that I trust him, I do trust him and I want to show him that I do, which can't happen if I stay downstairs through lack of trust.*

No, I'm going! (May 2, 1944)

Yet more than love was on Anne's mind that spring of 1944. The everlasting war was never far from her thoughts. *What, oh, what is the use of the war, why can't people live peacefully together, why all this destruction? . . . Oh why are people so crazy?* (May 3, 1944) Anne also wrote: *I am young and I possess many buried qualities . . . I have been given a lot, a*

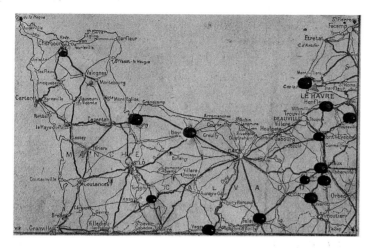

This is the map that Otto Frank pinned on the wall after the Allies landed in Normandy on June 6, 1944. The colored pins showed the progress of the Allied forces advancing through France. Every day for more than a year they had all hoped for this invasion. Now at last it was happening.

Could we be granted victory this year, this 1944? We don't know yet, but hope lives on; it gives us fresh courage, it makes us strong again. Since we must put up bravely with all the fears, privations, and sufferings, the great thing now is to remain calm and steadfast, now we must clench our teeth rather than cry out! . . .

Oh, Kitty, the best part of the invasion is that I have the feeling that friends are approaching. (June 6, 1944)

happy nature, a great deal of cheerfulness and strength. Every day I feel that I am developing inwardly, that the liberation is drawing nearer and how beautiful nature is, how good the people about me, how interesting and amusing this adventure! Why, then, should I be in despair? (May 3, 1944)

On June 6, 1944, the news of the Normandy invasion in France was on the radio! Anne was ecstatic. *Great commotion in the "Secret Annex." Would the long-awaited liberation about which so much has been said, but which still seems* too *wonderful,* too *much like a fairy tale, ever come true.* (June 6, 1944)

Anne celebrated her fifteenth birthday on June 12, six days after the Normandy invasion. The families had been in the Secret Annex for almost two years. Despite the massive invasion, the liberation of Europe still seemed a long way away, and life on the Prinsengracht went on as usual.

Anne had become disappointed in Peter. She had hoped he would become a good friend with whom she could talk about everything, but that hadn't really happened. Whether this was be-

Miep (seated) and Bep. The helpers knew that they were risking their lives to help their friends in hiding. Anne was also very aware of the danger they were in. On May 26, 1944, she wrote: *Miep and Kugler carry the heaviest burden of us and all those in hiding, Miep in all she does, and Kugler through the enormous responsibility for the 8 of us, which is sometimes so much for him that he can hardly talk from pent-up nerves and strain.*

cause he was still shy, or was slightly shallow, she didn't know, though she understood that the whole situation was as difficult for Peter as it was for her. Anne thought these times were much harder for young people than for adults. Older people were so sure about things. *It's twice as hard for us young ones to hold our ground, and maintain our opinions, in a time when all ideals are being shattered and destroyed, when people are showing their worst side, and do not know whether to believe in truth and right and in God. . . . That's the difficulty in these times, ideals, dreams and cherished hopes rise within us, only to meet the horrible truth and be shattered.*

It's really a wonder that I haven't dropped all my ideals, because they seem so absurd and impossible to carry out. Yet I keep them, because in spite of everything I still believe that people are really good at heart.

I simply can't build up my hopes on a foundation consisting of confusion, misery, and death, I see the world gradually being turned into a wilderness, I hear the ever approaching thunder, which will destroy us too, I can feel the sufferings of millions and yet, if I look up into the heavens, I think that it will all come right, that this cruelty too will end, and that peace and tranquility will return again. In the meantime, I must uphold my ideals, for perhaps the time will come when I shall be able to carry them out! (July 15, 1944)

On July 21, 1944, Anne was happy and optimistic. The news about the war seemed hopeful. Eleven days later, she made one last entry in her diary. On August 4 between ten o'clock and half past ten in the morning, the German police stormed the Secret Annex. They had been betrayed.

The Westertoren seen from the attic window of the Secret Annex.

Je Anne M. Frank.

Dinsdag, 1 Aug. 1944.

Lieve Kitty,

This is the last entry that Anne made in her diary, Tuesday, August 1, 1944. Anne wrote that she thought it was a shame that the others in the Secret Annex only really knew one side of her. She was often berated and criticized for that side, and not taken seriously by the adults because of it. *I have already told you before that I have, as it were, a dual personality. One half embodies my exuberant cheerfulness, making fun of everything, vivacity, and above all the way I take everything lightly. . . . This side is usually lying in wait and pushes away the other, which is much better, deeper and purer. No one knows Anne's better side.*

Three days after Anne wrote this, the German police entered the Secret Annex.

The Diary Is Left Behind

It was a beautiful, hot summer's day, a day like any other. As usual, Otto Frank went to Peter's room in the morning to give him an English lesson. Otto looked at his watch: almost half past ten, time to start teaching.

At that moment Peter raised his hand. He looked frightened. From downstairs they heard noises, strange men's voices, shouting, threatening voices . . .

A few minutes earlier, five men had suddenly entered the office building. One of them was wearing the uniform of the German police. The others were in civilian clothes, and were probably Dutch Nazis. Miep, Bep, Johannes Kleiman, and Victor Kugler were in the office.

Karl Silberbauer, the police officer who arrested the families in the Secret Annex.

Johannes Kleiman next to the book-case, after the war.

The five men knew everything. Victor Kugler had to take them upstairs. When they got to the bookcase, the men drew their revolvers. They opened the secret door and went inside.

A minute later one of the Dutch Nazis went into Peter's room, pointing his revolver at him. Otto and Peter went downstairs. There they saw all the others with their hands raised, including Anne and Margot. Karl Silberbauer, the officer, barked out an abrupt demand for money and jewelry. He grabbed a briefcase and emptied out its contents; the papers from Anne's diaries fell to the floor. He put the money and jewelry into the briefcase. Karl Silberbauer did not believe that they had all been hiding in the Secret Annex for more than two years. Then Otto Frank showed him the marks on the wall, where Anne's and Margot's heights had been measured.

On August 4, 1944, the eight people who had been hiding in the Secret Annex were taken in a covered truck to this German police station, which was located in two schools commandeered by the Germans. The day after their arrest, they were transferred to another building and put in a holding cell.

Some of the Frank family's photo albums, which Miep Gies managed to save from the Secret Annex, along with Anne's diary and a number of schoolbooks.

The eight prisoners were allowed to pack a few clothes. Then they were taken in a truck to a German police station. Victor Kugler and Johannes Kleiman were also arrested and taken with them. (Later they were interned in a camp. Both survived.)

Now it was quiet on the Prinsengracht. Miep and Bep had not been taken away, though they feared that the men would come back to arrest them at any moment. At the end of the afternoon, the two went upstairs together with Jan Gies and Van Maaren, the warehouseman, and entered the Secret Annex. It was in chaos. The pages of Anne's diary lay scattered on the floor and were gathered up along with other papers and books and taken downstairs. The Frank family's photo albums were also retrieved. Miep put the pages of the diary in her desk drawer and locked it. About a week later the whole Secret Annex was emptied on German orders.

Who betrayed the hiding place to the Germans remains a mystery to this day.

The family spent four days locked in a holding cell. Then on August 8 they were transferred to the Westerbork camp. They stayed there for the whole of the month of August in the so-called "punishment barracks." They were considered "punishable prisoners" since they had not given themselves up when the call-up notices were sent but had been captured in hiding.

On September 3, 1944, the eight prisoners joined a thousand others on the last train bound for the Auschwitz death camp in Poland. They were cooped up in a boxcar for days, crammed together with about seventy other people, and arrived in Auschwitz on the night of September 5. More than half of the people were killed in the gas chambers the very next day, including nearly all the children under fifteen. Since Anne had just had her fifteenth birthday, she was spared. The men and women were separated, most never to see each other again. The women had to walk to the women's camp in Birkenau. Edith Frank and her two daughters stayed together. Mrs. Van Pels also went to the women's camp.

Otto Frank, Hermann and Peter van Pels, and Fritz Pfeffer went to the men's camp.

The conditions in Auschwitz were indescribably wretched. The prisoners were given hardly anything to eat and no medicines were available. Hundreds died from starvation and illness every day. The guards beat and clubbed people to death for no reason at all. Every day new groups of prisoners were sent to the gas chambers. No

The Germans completely emptied the houses of Jews who had been captured and deported. Anything of value was sent to Germany. The company hired by the Germans to strip the houses in Amsterdam was the Puls company, whose name can be seen on the side of these trucks. This is why the people of Amsterdam referred to "pulsing" a house.

Westerbork, like all the concentration camps, was highly overcrowded. Every week a freight train left there with more than a thousand men, women, and children for one of the death camps, camps which had been specifically designed for mass murder. The eight people from the Secret Annex were on the last train that left Westerbork for Auschwitz.

The platform at Auschwitz-Birkenau. This is where the families from the Secret Annex arrived, and where the "selection" took place. People who were strong enough to work for the Germans were allowed to live—at least for a little while. Most of the others, including children under fifteen, went straight to the gas chambers. Anne escaped this fate since she had just had her fifteenth birthday.

one could be sure of his or her life. Every day could be the last.

Hermann van Pels was murdered in the gas chambers a couple of weeks after his arrival in Auschwitz-Birkenau. Fritz Pfeffer ended up in the Neuengamme concentration camp, where he died on December 20, 1944.

The Russian Army was approaching from the east; the other Allied forces that had landed in

France were approaching from the west. The Germans knew that they had lost the war. Many of the camps were cleared and dismantled in an effort to erase the evidence of their crimes. Prisoners were shot and buried in mass graves. Others were transferred to concentration camps farther from the front.

5	Judentransport aus den Niederlanden — Lager Westerbork			Blatt 7
	3.September			
	am Häeftlinge		194 .	
3o1. Engers	Isidor	3o.4. 93	Kaufmann	
3o2. Engers	Leonard	13.6. 2o	Landerbeiter	
3o3. Franco	Manfred	1.5. o5	Verleger	
3o4. Frank	Arthur	22.8. 81	Kaufmann	
3o5. Frank	Isaac	29.11.87	Installateur	
3o6. Frank	Margot	16.2. 26	ohne	
3o7. Frank	Otto	12.5. 89	Kaufmann	
3o8. Frank-Hollaender	Edith	16.1. oo	ohne	
3o9. Frank	Anneliese	12.6. 29	ohne	
31o. v.Franck	Sara	27.4. o2	Typistin	
311. Franken	Abraham	16.5. 96	Landarbeiter	
312. Franken-Weyand	Johanna	24.12.96	Landbauer	
313. Franken	Hermann	12.5. 34	ohne	
314. Franken	Louis	1o.8. 17	Gaertner	
315. Franken	Rosalina	29.3. 27	Landbau	
316. Frankfort	Alex	14.11.19	Dr.i.d.Oekonomie	
317. Frankfort-Elzas	Regina	11.12.19	Apoth.-Ass.	
318. Frankfoort	Elias	22.1o.98	Schneider	
319. Frankfort	Max	2o.8. 21	Schneider	
32o. Frankfort-Weijl	Betty	25.3. 24	Näeherin	
321. Frankfort-Jerkendam	Rozette	24.6. 98	Schriftstellerin	
322. Frijda	Herman	22.6. 87	Hochschullehrer	
323. Frenk	Henriette	28.4. 21	Typistin	

The list of names of people on the last transport from Westerbork to Auschwitz, including the names of the Frank family.

THE MAJOR CONCENTRATION AND DEATH CAMPS

The first concentration camps were built in Germany soon after Hitler came to power in 1933. Here all those opposed to Hitler—political adversaries, members of the Resistance, people considered inferior by the Nazis—were "concentrated" in highly fortified camps. Many prisoners were shot, or died of hunger, disease, or exhaustion.

After the invasion of Poland in the fall of 1939 and of the Soviet Union in June 1941, hundreds of thousands of captured Jews were shot on the spot. Then in the beginning of 1942, the Nazis decided to launch a campaign of systematic murder against the Jews of Europe. Concentration camps designed for killing on a mass scale were built in Poland. The Nazis called these "extermination camps."

By the end of the Second World War the Nazis succeeded in murdering about 6 million Jews.

This map shows the estimated number of Jews killed in different countries. Not shown are the death tolls for the Jews of Norway (728), Finland (11), Estonia (1,000), Greece (71,300), Albania (200), and Libya (562).

Camps that Held the People from the Secret Annex

Auschwitz-Birkenau: All eight people who had been hiding in the Secret Annex were taken here in September 1944. Hermann van Pels was gassed to death a few weeks later. Edith Frank died here on January 6, 1945. At the end of January 1945, the Russian

SWED
(Neut

DENMARK
77

THE NETHERLANDS
106,000

NEUENGAMME

RAV

BERGEN-
BELSEN

SACHS

GERMANY
160,000

VUGHT

DORA-MITTELBAU

BUCHENWALD

BELGIUM
24,000

TH

LUXEMBOURG
700

FLOSSENBÜRG

FRANCE
83,000

NATZWEILER

DACHAU

SWITZERLAND
(Neutral)

ITALY
8,000

LATVIA
80,000

LITHUANIA
135,000

STUTTHOF

▲ TREBLINKA
▬▬▬▬▬▬▬▬

POLAND
3,000,000

▲ CHELMNO
▬▬▬▬▬▬▬▬

▲ SOBIBOR

▲ MAIDANEK
▬▬▬▬▬▬▬▬

▲ BELZEC
▬▬▬▬▬▬▬▬

SS-ROSEN

Ⓐ AUSCHWITZ-BIRKENAU
▬▬▬▬▬▬▬▬▬▬▬▬▬

CZECHOSLOVAKIA
277,000

ᴜSEN

HUNGARY
305,000

ROMANIA
365,000

YUGOSLAVIA
67,000

THE SOVIET UNION
1,000,000

Army liberated the camp. Otto Frank survived.

Mauthausen: Peter van Pels was transferred here from Auschwitz-Birkenau. He died on May 5, 1945, three days before the camp was liberated.

Bergen-Belsen: Anne and Margot Frank and Mrs. Van Pels were moved to this camp in October 1944. Anne and Margot died here in March 1945. The camp was liberated the following month.

Buchenwald: After a short time in Bergen-Belsen, Mrs. Van Pels was transferred here briefly before being moved again.

Theresienstadt: This is the last camp where Mrs. Van Pels was imprisoned. She probably died here in the spring of 1945.

Neuengamme: Fritz Pfeffer was transferred to this camp from Auschwitz-Birkenau. He died here on December 20, 1944.

KEY

▲ **concentration camps**

▬▬▬ **death camps**

▬▬▬ **estimated number of Jews killed per country**

Ⓐ **camps where the people from the Secret Annex were imprisoned**

The countries on this map are drawn with their 1939 borders.

95

The Murder of Millions

The Nazis declared that the German people were a super-race, and that there was no place in their empire for people they considered inferior, a list which included gypsies, blacks, homosexuals, handicapped people, and Jews.

In January 1942, the leadership of the Nazi Party decided to murder more than 11 million Jews then in Europe—simply because they were Jews. To this end, they built extermination camps. These were concentration camps specially designed for the fast and efficient execution of millions. The death camps were all run by the "Death's Head" S.S., so called for the skull insignia on their caps and their talents for torture and cruelty. These camps were built in total secrecy in isolated areas of Poland: Auschwitz-Birkenau (the largest death camp), Treblinka, Belzec, Sobibor, Chelmno, and Maidanek. No one was to know the real reason the Jews were deported here. The Nazis claimed that the Jews were simply being taken to work camps in Poland. Most people believed the lie.

Gypsy children from a German children's home. Shortly after this photograph was taken, they were transported to Auschwitz and murdered.

Trains from every European country under German occupation went back and forth to Poland carrying Jews crowded together in cattle cars. The journey could take days, with nothing given to the prisoners to eat or drink, and no word said about what was to become of them. Most trains went straight to the death camps. Most people were murdered in the gas chambers a few hours after arriving, their bodies then burned in huge incinerators. For a while the Nazis spared those people they thought they could use. Yet even these strong young men and women had to work so incredibly hard for the Germans, under such wretched conditions, that most died within a few weeks. A few very lucky ones were still alive when the Allied Forces liberated the camps in 1945. Altogether, roughly 6 million Jews were murdered. The great majority of gypsies who had been deported to the camps from the occupied countries also did not survive the war.

People being transported in cattle cars to the camps.

When Anne, Margot, and their mother arrived in Auschwitz-Birkenau, their heads were shaved and numbers were tattooed on their arms. About 39,000 women were in this camp.

Anne and Margot had to leave their mother behind in Auschwitz at the end of October 1944. Like Mrs. Van Pels, the two girls were transferred to the concentration camp at Bergen-Belsen. There, too, the conditions were indescribable. It was icy cold and there was hardly anything to eat. The camp was overcrowded and contagious diseases spread unchecked.

Edith Frank survived in Auschwitz for another two months. She died on January 6, 1945.

Peter van Pels, like most other prisoners, was transferred from Auschwitz to the Mauthausen camp in Austria by the S.S. on January 16. This was ten days before the Russian Army liberated Auschwitz. Peter died in Mauthausen on May 5, 1945.

Mrs. Van Pels was in Bergen-Belsen only for a short while before being transferred to Theresienstadt via Buchenwald. She died there in the spring of 1945.

Margot and Anne struggled to survive in Bergen-Belsen. They slept in an unheated bar-

Photographs of the camp at Bergen-Belsen taken just after its liberation. For the last few months before the liberation in April 1945, Bergen-Belsen was extremely overcrowded. Most of the inmates were women, jammed together in barracks where contagious diseases raged.

The conditions in Bergen-Belsen were so bad that tens of thousands of people died. Anne and Margot died a few weeks before the camp was liberated by the British Army.

racks crammed with women. Some women who survived would later report seeing and talking to Anne and Margot.

"I saw Anne and her sister again in the barracks . . ." said Mrs. Van Amerongen-Frankfoorder. "The Frank girls were almost unrecognizable since their hair had been cut off. . . . And they were cold."

Lies Goosen, an old school friend of Anne's, turned out to be in another part of the camp. She talked to Anne through the barbed wire. "It was so terrible. She immediately began to cry, and she told me, 'I don't have any parents anymore.' . . . I always think, if Anne had known that her father was still alive, she might have had more strength to survive."

Mrs. Brandes-Brilleslijper related: "She told me that she had such a horror of the lice and fleas in her clothes and that she had thrown all of her clothes away. It was the middle of winter and she was wrapped in one blanket."

Mrs. Van Amerongen-Frankfoorder saw the girls again. "The Frank girls were so emaciated. They looked terrible. . . . it was clear that they had typhus. You could really see both of them dying."

Margot died in March 1945. A few days later, Anne died as well. The camp was liberated by British soldiers a few weeks later in April.

Otto Frank was the only one of the group from the Secret Annex to survive the war. He was still in Auschwitz when the Russians liberated the

When the Allied forces liberated the remaining Jews in the concentration camps in Germany and Poland, they could hardly believe the horror they saw. Now the survivors' difficult journey home began. Most had lost all their family and friends. When they returned home, their stories were often not believed, or their listeners were not interested. Only 4,700 Jews returned to the Netherlands from the camps.

camp on January 27, 1945. He wanted to go back to Amsterdam, but the war had not ended yet in the Netherlands. Otto started the long journey home to Amsterdam on March 5, 1945. The Russians took him and a group of other survivors to the port of Odessa on the Black Sea. From Odessa, he went by boat to Marseilles in France, and continued by train and truck to Amsterdam.

This photograph was taken in 1951, when Otto Frank was living with Miep and Jan Gies. In 1952 he moved to Basel. A year later he married Elfriede Geiringer.

Otto Frank did not arrive in Amsterdam until June 3, when he immediately went to see Miep and Jan Gies.

Their reunion was filled with joy and sadness. Otto Frank said he had heard that his wife, Edith, was dead, but he still hoped that Anne and Margot were alive. He had heard that they had been taken to Bergen-Belsen, and that at least Bergen-Belsen was not a death camp. Otto moved in with Miep and Jan, and together they searched daily for news about Anne and Margot.

Almost two months later Otto received word that both his daughters had died.

All this time Miep had kept Anne's diaries, hoping to give them back to Anne herself. As it was now certain that Anne was dead, Miep got out the diaries and gave them to Otto. Otto started reading them immediately and was moved and astonished. He had never realized that Anne had recorded everything that happened in the Secret Annex so well and so accurately. Otto typed large parts of the diary in German and sent them to his mother in Switzerland.

Later he let other people read parts of the diary. They urged him to look for a publisher, but no one wanted to publish the diary so soon after the war. It was only when an article appeared on Anne's diaries in the Dutch newspaper *Het Parool (The Motto)* on April 3, 1946, that a publisher was found. Anne Frank's diary was published in an edition of 1,500 copies in the summer of 1947.

Otto had now fulfilled Anne's wish to become a writer.

The diary was soon translated into French and then into German. In 1951, an English edition was published. In the years that followed, the diary was translated into thirty-one other languages.

The diary became world-famous. Now, more than forty-five years later, the book has been pub-

The Dutch Red Cross did not issue an official declaration of Anne Frank's death until 1954. This paper confirmed that Anne Frank had died in Bergen-Belsen in 1945. There was also a declaration of death for Margot.

lished in fifty-five languages, more than 20 million copies have been sold, and plays and films based on the book have been produced. Throughout the world, streets and schools have been named after Anne Frank.

For many people Anne Frank became a symbol of the six million Jewish men, women, and children who were murdered by the Nazis in the Second World War. It is almost impossible to comprehend this number, but the story of Anne Frank makes it possible to understand what the war meant for one of these victims.

Otto Frank spent the rest of his life spreading Anne's ideas and ideals. In 1979, one year before his death, he wrote: "Anne never spoke about hatred anywhere in her diary. She wrote that despite everything, she believed in the goodness of people. And that when the war was over, she wanted to work for the world and for people.

Like many of the Jews who returned home after the war, Otto Frank placed a notice in the newspaper in the "Information requested about" column. On August 1, 1945, this entry appeared: "MARGOT FRANK (19) and ANNA FRANK (16) in Jan. on trans. from Bergen-Belsen. O. Frank, Prinsengracht 263, tel. 37059."

Some of the many translated editions of the diary of Anne Frank.

This is the duty I have taken over from her. I have received many thousands of letters. Young people especially always want to know how these terrible things could ever have happened. I answer them as well as I can, and I often finish by saying: 'I hope that Anne's book will have an effect on the rest of your life so that insofar as it is possible in your circumstances, you will work for unity and peace.' "

Otto Frank in 1967. Otto died in Birsfelden, a suburb of Basel, on August 19, 1980, at the age of ninety-one. He donated the pages of Anne's diary to the State of the Netherlands.

On April 3, 1946, this article titled "Kinderstem" ("A Child's Voice") appeared in the newspaper *Het Parool*. In his article, Professor Jan Romein wrote about Anne's diary: "By coincidence I came across a diary that was written during the war. The Netherlands State Institute for War Documentation already has about 200 of such diaries, but it would surprise me if there was one other which was as pure, as intelligent and yet as human as this one."

Anne Frank House

Anne Frank's room. There is no longer any furniture in the Secret Annex, but many traces of the families who lived there in hiding remain, such as these photographs of movie stars which Anne put up on the walls.

You've known for a long time that my greatest wish is to become . . . a famous writer. (Anne Frank, May 11, 1944)

Anne Frank's wish was fulfilled after her death. People throughout the world have read Anne's diary and, because it captured so well the feelings and experiences of one of the war's many victims, have made Anne Frank a symbol of the millions of Jews who perished in the Second World War. Moreover, Anne has become a symbol for all people who are persecuted today for their background, the color of their skin, or their beliefs.

After the war, the house where the Frank family had gone into hiding, number 263 Prinsengracht in Amsterdam, continued to be used as a business office. By 1957, it had fallen into such disrepair that there were plans to demolish it. Many people opposed the demolition, some of whom joined Otto Frank in setting up the Anne Frank House in Amsterdam.

They succeeded in saving the building, which was opened to the public in 1960. Visitors to the premises of numbers 263 and 265 Prinsengracht can not only see the Secret Annex, but can also view exhibitions set up throughout the building on anti-Semitism, the history and ideology of the Nazis, and the Netherlands during the Second World War, as well as a display of the original diaries of Anne Frank. Attention is also given to contemporary examples of intolerance, racism, discrimination, and anti-Semitism.

The Anne Frank House in Amsterdam. Every year it is visited by about 600,000 people from all over the world.

Chronology

Chronology of the Frank Family and the Families in the Secret Annex

May 12, 1889: Otto Frank is born in Frankfurt am Main, Germany.

January 16, 1900: Edith Holländer is born in Aachen, Germany.

May 12, 1925: Otto Frank and Edith Holländer are married.

February 16, 1926: Margot Frank is born in Frankfurt am Main.

Autumn 1927: The Frank family moves to their new home at number 307 Marbachweg.

June 12, 1929: Anne Frank is born in Frankfurt am Main.

March 1931: The Frank family moves to number 24 Ganghoferstrasse.

Summer 1933: Edith, Margot, and Anne Frank go to stay with Grandmother Holländer in Aachen. Otto Frank looks for their home in Amsterdam, the Netherlands.

September 15, 1933: Otto Frank establishes the company Opekta-Works.

October 1933: Alice Frank-Stern, Anne's grandmother, moves to Basel, Switzerland.

December 5, 1933: Edith and Margot Frank move to Amsterdam.

February 1934: Anne Frank moves to Amsterdam.

1934: Anne begins her Montessori schooling.

Summer 1937: The Van Pels family flees Osnabrück, Germany, for the Netherlands.

June 1, 1938: Otto Frank establishes his second company, Pectacon B. V.

December 8, 1938: Fritz Pfeffer flees Germany for the Netherlands.

March 1939: Grandmother Holländer moves from Aachen to live with the Frank family.

December 1, 1940: Otto Frank's company moves to number 263 on the Prinsengracht Canal in Amsterdam.

May 8, 1941: Opekta-Works changes its name to Trading Company Gies & Co.

Summer 1941: Anne and Margot attend the Jewish Lyceum in Amsterdam.

January 1942: Grandmother Holländer dies.

June 12, 1942: Anne Frank receives the diary for her thirteenth birthday.

July 5, 1942: Margot Frank receives a notice ordering her to report for deportation to the Westerbork camp.

July 6, 1942: The Frank family goes into hiding in the Secret Annex at number 263 Prinsengracht.

July 13, 1942: The Van Pels family (Van Daan in the diary) join the Frank family in the Secret Annex.

November 16, 1942: Fritz Pfeffer (Albert Dussel in the diary) moves into the Secret Annex.

August 4, 1944: The families hiding in the Secret Annex are discovered.

August 8, 1944: The people from the Secret Annex

are transported to the concentration camp at Westerbork.

September 3, 1944: The prisoners are sent to the concentration camp at Auschwitz in Poland.

September 6, 1944: They arrive in Auschwitz. Hermann van Pels dies here a few weeks later.

October 1944: Anne and Margot are taken to the concentration camp at Bergen-Belsen.

December 20, 1944: Fritz Pfeffer dies in Neuengamme.

January 6, 1945: Edith Frank dies in Auschwitz.

January 27, 1945: Otto Frank is freed when Auschwitz is liberated by the Russian Army.

March 1945: Anne and Margot Frank die in Bergen-Belsen.

May 5, 1945: Peter van Pels dies in Mauthausen.

Spring 1945: Mrs. Van Pels dies in Theresienstadt.

June 3, 1945: Otto Frank returns to Amsterdam.

Summer 1947: The diary of Anne Frank is published in Dutch.

1952: Otto Frank moves to Basel, Switzerland.

November 1953: Otto Frank marries Elfriede Geiringer.

August 19, 1980: Otto Frank dies in Birsfelden at the age of ninety-one.

The Helpers

Bep Voskuijl died on May 6, 1983. Victor Kugler moved to Toronto, Canada, in 1955; he died there on December 16, 1981. Johannes Kleiman died on January 30, 1959. Jan Gies died on January 26, 1993. Miep Gies is still living in Amsterdam.

Notes on the Different Versions of the Diary of Anne Frank

In the spring of 1944, Anne Frank heard Minister Bolkestein on *Radio Oranje* saying that the Dutch government was planning to collect diaries and letters about the war for publication after the war's end. A few weeks after hearing this broadcast, Anne began editing her diary, hoping it would be published one day. She copied her diary onto single sheets of paper, cutting out and rewriting parts and making some additions. While making her revisions, Anne also continued to write entries in her regular diary. The authors used Anne's revised text for most of the diary entries in this book. Anne's revisions stopped after March 24, 1944; all entries after this date are from Anne's original diary.

After the war, Miep Gies gave the loose sheets of the revision and the original diaries to Otto Frank. After considerable thought, Otto Frank decided to publish the diary. He typed a manuscript using both the original diary and the version Anne revised. He left out some entries which he thought unimportant or uninteresting. He also changed the names of the people in hiding and the helpers, following a list that Anne had drawn up when she was working on her revision. The false names Anne devised are given below, followed by the real names:

Mr. Koophuis—
    Johannes Kleiman
Mr. Kraler—Victor Kugler
Elli Vossen—Bep Voskuijl
Mr. Vossen—Mr. Voskuijl
Miep van Santen—
    Miep Gies
Henk van Santen—
    Jan Gies
The Van Daan family—
    the Van Pels family
Albert Dussel—
    Fritz Pfeffer

The diary was first published in Holland in 1947 as *Het Achterhuis (The Secret Annex)*. It was published in the United States in 1952 as *Anne Frank: The Diary of a Young Girl.*

Otto Frank died in 1980, leaving all the papers and original books of his daughter's diary to the State of the Netherlands. These papers were all submitted to a scientific examination to prove the diary's authenticity. Beginning in the 1950s, increasing numbers of people had insisted that the diary was a fake, arguing that no child of fifteen could possibly have produced such a well-written book. These rumors were dispelled once and for all when the examination proved beyond doubt that the diary was authentic. The results of the examination were published in Holland in 1986 in *The Diaries of Anne Frank*, and in the United States in 1988 in *The Diary of Anne Frank: The Critical Edition*. In addition to the test results, this book contains almost all the different diary texts, as well as information on the Frank family's background, their life in hiding, and their betrayal.

Sources of Quotations and Photographs

Quotations

All quotations of the diary of Anne Frank: The Netherlands State Institute for War Documentation, *The Diary of Anne Frank: The Critical Edition.* Edited by David Barnouw and Gerrold van der Stroom; translated by Arnold J. Pomerans and B. M. Mooyaart-Doubleday (New York: Doubleday, 1989).

Page 69: Anne Frank, *Anne Frank's Tales from the Secret Annex* (Middlesex: Penguin, 1986), p. 25.

Pages 100–101: Willy Lindwer, *The Last Seven Months of Anne Frank* (New York: Pantheon, 1991):
  Mrs. Van Amerongen-Frankfoorder: pp. 103–104
  Mrs. Pick-Gosler (Lies Goosen): pp. 27–28
  Mrs. Brandes-Brilleslijper: p. 74

Pages 104–105, the quotation of Otto Frank: Anne Frank Stiftung, *Anne Frank 1929–1979* (Heidelberg: Verlag Lambert Scheider, 1979), p. 63.

All texts by Anne Frank copyright © Anne Frank Fonds, Basel

Photographs

© ANP-foto: p. 81
Gemeentearchief Amsterdam: pp. 22 *(top)*, 43.
Miep Gies: pp. 25 *(bottom)*, 32 *(right)*, 34, 41 *(top)*, 60.
Historisches Museum Frankfurt am Main: pp. 8 *(right)*, 13.
© Wubbo de Jong: pp. 52, 57, 63 *(bottom)*.
© Jules Huf: p. 87 *(top)*.
© KLM Luchtfotografie-Schiphol: p. 49.
© Vereniging Lau Mazirel: p. 96.
© Marius Meijboom: p. 70.
© Cas Oorthuys/Stichting Nederlands Fotoarchief: p. 54.

Opekta Werke: p. 26 *(top)*.
Rijksinstituut voor Oorlogs-documentatie: pp. 16, 20, 31, 44, 45, 55, 71, 88, 91 *(both)*, 92 *(both)*, 97, 98, 99 *(both)*, 100 *(both)*, 101.
Rode Kruis, The Hague: p. 93.
© Spaarnestad Fotoarchief: pp. 15, 19, 30 *(bottom)*.
Stedelijk Beheer Amsterdam: p. 46 *(map)*.
© Stichting Particam/Maria Austria: pp. 48, 59 *(both)*, 61, 66, 72, 75, 78, 79, 87 *(bottom)*.

All other photographs are from the collection of the Anne Frank House, © AFF/Anne Frank House, Amsterdam. The Anne Frank House has tried to contact those people who have the copyright to photographs. Anyone who believes he or she has a copyright to illustrations and/or text is requested to contact the Anne Frank House.

Index of People
and Places